The War of 1812

The War of 1812

VICTOR SUTHREN

M&S

Canadian Cataloguing in Publication Data

Suthren, Victor, 1942-
The War of 1812

ISBN 0-7710-8317-3

1. Canada – History – War of 1812.*
2. United States – History – War of 1812. I. Title.

FC 442.S97 1999   971.03'4   C99-931375-4
E354.S97 1999

We acknowledge the financial support of the Government of Canada through
the Book Publishing Industry Development Program for our publishing activities.

We further acknowledge the support of the Canada Council for the Arts
and the Ontario Arts Council for our publishing program.
Canada

Book design: Ingrid Paulson
Typeset in New Baskerville by M&S, Toronto
Printed and bound in Canada

McClelland & Stewart Inc.
The Canadian Publishers
481 University Avenue
Toronto, Ontario
M5G 2E9

1 2 3 4 5   03 02 01 00 99

CONTENTS

ACKNOWLEDGEMENTS

The author wishes to thank Pat Kennedy for her patient and meticulous guidance and editing, Lisan Jutras for her copyediting, and Janet Torge for her determined and endlessly painstaking work as picture researcher. He also wishes to thank Brian McKenna, Andrea Nemtin, and Arnie Gelbart for believing that he could write a good story, and McClelland & Stewart for agreeing with them.

CHAPTER ONE

"An awful and eventful contest"

TRIUMPH AND LOSS IN THE FIRST YEAR

*I*T IS A LARGELY FORGOTTEN WAR NOW. Freeways and concrete towers have replaced dark forests or ploughed fields where hard men fought desperately with tomahawk and flintlock between the years 1812 and 1814. Bulk carriers and yachts track through waters where squadrons of sailing warships thundered broadsides at one another. The thousand-mile theatre of the ferocious and bloody struggle of the War of 1812 now throngs with commerce and with burgeoning cities whose inhabitants have little awareness of the butchery and destruction that made firm the unguarded borders dividing them – borders now crossed in daily business and tourism. The bodies of the war's victims and heroes alike, in red or blue cloth or in native buckskin, lie largely forgotten under the concrete and commerce, and to paraphrase the words of the Canadian folksinger Stan Rogers, not one in ten thousand knows their names.

School curricula in North America turn away increasingly from history, and in the lands that straddle and surround the Great Lakes and the Ohio and St. Lawrence River valleys, little is taught of the last war that happened there. For American students, if the War of 1812 is recalled at all, it is as a time of naval success against a bullying Royal Navy, and Andrew Jackson's storybook defence of New Orleans. There is little memory of defeats in disastrous campaigns against Canada, or the humiliation of the burning of Washington. In a healing but selective recollection there is focus instead on Francis Scott Key, writing of the British "rockets' red glare" illuminating a defiant American flag over a heroic Fort McHenry at Baltimore, rather than on the collapse of national defence that allowed a British fleet and army to sail at will in American waters.

For Canadian students, even the reasons for such a bitter struggle are as difficult to comprehend as the events of the war itself. If the story is addressed at all, it has tended until recent years to perpetuate a myth of resolute Canadian militiamen, farmers, and shopkeepers, hurling back the republican hordes from the south, aided by the British army and an indistinct Indian participation. There is little awareness that most of the fighting on Canada's behalf was done by tiny forces of exhausted British soldiers and the warriors of an Indian alliance that was fighting for its last chance at meaningful survival.

Each society has chosen what it wants to believe of the forgotten war, to strengthen its sense of national identity; each is unaware of the degree to which the thousand-mile struggle shaped not only the character of each country, but also their joint relationship. And neither Canada nor the United States seems sufficiently aware that the disparate Indian nations of the Old Northwest, which fought and gave so much in the struggle, received in the war a death blow to their identity as a social and political power – from both the American soldiery and the abandonment of their cause by Britain in the peace treaty that followed.

For Great Britain, of which the Canadas, Upper and Lower, were a colony, the war remains a footnote, a seldom-mentioned sideshow to the huge and sprawling struggle against the French known as the Napoleonic Wars, which exhausted Britain of men and resources from 1792 to 1815, with only brief intermissions. In 1812 the British still had the glory of the Victorian Empire awaiting them and, as that broad grandeur unfolded, the memory of a distant, irritating, and inconclusive war had little interest. Yet, if attended to, there were lessons on the limitations of power inherent in the struggle – and intimations of where new power would ultimately emerge.

A variety of reasons led the young United States to declare war on Great Britain on June 18, 1812, but ultimately they reduced down to international issues and North American ones. And at the heart of both lay a perception on the part of the adolescent republic that they were dismissed as a people, and as a society, and were not granted respect by the British government and nation. If moderate Americans faced any serious objection to their worries about what war might do to things like trade, it arose from this:

British Surrender at Yorktown, 1781. *The surrender of Cornwallis's army and the peace treaty that followed in 1783 did not earn the United States the respect they had expected from the British.*

a demand for dignity raised by other Americans and a need for self-respect to counter a perceived lack of recognition from a preoccupied and indifferent Great Britain. The roots of this feeling, of course, lay in the American Revolution, which had ended by peace treaty in 1783, and which had nominally brought forth on the North American continent a new nation independent of the United Kingdom.

In the seventeenth and eighteenth centuries, North America was the setting for a vast struggle for empire between France and Britain. The French had established themselves along the St. Lawrence River Valley, and from there had spread a claim of sovereignty over much of the interior of North America, including south into the Ohio Valley. The English settlements lay along the east coast, shut in behind the Appalachian Mountains. Far more numerous than the French in their snug settlements of the St. Lawrence, the English colonists were developing an independent frame of mind, even while they remained dependent on the forces of the British Crown to defend them from the French; they soon tested this independence in a quest for more territory. But as the "Americans" – as the colonists were increasingly coming to be known – began to press through the Appalachian mountain chain in the 1750s, they naturally came into conflict with the French. Elsewhere, Britain and France were continuing their renewed rivalry in a series of wars that had begun in 1692, and the friction between American colonists and the French in the lush Ohio Valley finally precipitated an open war in North America, which spread to a global conflict. Britain called it the "Seven Years' War," since it was fought from 1756 to 1763; the American colonists called it the "French and Indian War," because for them it was a war not only against the French, but against their Indian allies, who bitterly opposed the growth and migration westward of American settlement across the mountains.

The attitude of the French and the British towards the indigenous nations of North America had led, in part, to this state of affairs. The French were less interested in the wholesale shipment of a population to North America than they were in working in harmony with the native tribes in order to preserve a profitable trade in furs, and to allow a blending of French and Indian culture that might lead in time to a Christianized society loyal to the king of France. By design or instinct, the French society of New France – once a time of war with the Iroquois in the seventeenth

Canoes in a Fog, by Frances Ann Hopkins. The fur trade was the lifeblood of New France, and it stayed a vital part of the economy of British North America until the decline in European demand for beaver pelts in hat-making after 1821. Great canoes such as these were the communication link in early Canada from the St. Lawrence to the head of the Great Lakes and beyond.

century had passed – had been open to that of the Indian. There was an ease of integration, a willingness to intermarry and absorb aspects of Indian thought and culture, which made the Frenchman far more the ally and friend of the Indian than was the English settler. Whether this was because France desired the hearts of the tribes rather than their hunting lands remains debatable; it was less debatable that the English-speaking population in North America was implacably hostile to Native society. For the Americans, there were increasingly fewer links back across the Atlantic, no market or master elsewhere across the seas to be served. North America was to be the place where his society and his culture would flourish, and his vision was of a freehold agrarian yeomanry, where independent farmers hacked a new life out of a dark and threatening wilderness. There was far less a desire for lucrative trade with the Indian than there was for land, for farms, for the opportunity to raise children and crops by beating back an uncivil savagery. To all this there was a strangely tribal quality of uncompromising determination, perhaps arising from the dark inheritances in the Scottish–Irish origins of so many of the settlers. Joined with the speculative land hunger of wealthier colonial families – who were also eyeing the Ohio Valley – it made war with the French and their Indian allies virtually inevitable.

The soldiery packed in their landing barges make their way towards the Anse du Foulon during the siege of Quebec. Britain's ability to combine land and sea forces spelled defeat for French efforts to retain New France.

The war was fought with horrifying savagery and ended with Britain's victory and the Treaty of Paris in 1763. In a stroke, the British had taken possession of a continent – with the exception of territories owned by Spain – leaving a remnant French population that had been abandoned by their upper classes, which had returned to France. From Florida to Hudson Bay, the unimaginable riches of North America now belonged to George III and his subjects. But the very removal of the French threat – though not the Indian one – to the survival of the English colonies now allowed the growing distance to widen between the independent-minded colonists and the remote government in the British Isles. (There were also existing irritations: in 1749, for example, as part of a treaty with France ending the war of 1739–1748, Britain had returned the French fortified port of Louisbourg, in Nova Scotia, to France in exchange for cessions in India. The place had been taken with great effort and zeal – and casualties – by an amateur army of "American" colonists, who now saw their concerns and efforts set aside because of Britain's wider interests.) A body of issues arose, ranging from a sense of unfair taxation to anger at a British act of 1774 that appeared to pen the English colonists behind the Appalachians and reserve the Ohio lands for the Indians and the profit of fur traders in Quebec. Confrontation overcame conciliation, and in the Revolutionary War rebel-

The Death of General Wolfe, Quebec. *This later rendering (1857) suggests the close tumult of the battle. The British victory led to the end of the French threat in North America, and to a widening distance between Britain and its North American colonies.*

lious colonists overcame both their loyalist countrymen and the British Army to earn independence by treaty in 1783. The fact that the victory had been won because of a large measure of good fortune, British uncertainty, and a French alliance did not take away from a sense of nationhood won.

In the years following the war, however, it was soon evident to the Americans that the United Kingdom viewed the divorce as neither irrevocable nor worthy of serious respect; "Jonathan," as the American was called, did not have in British eyes the status of a respected foreign national, and this humiliation burned deep behind the motivations of many who would later, in 1812, urge the United States towards war with Britain. Had the British government, locked in the climactic struggle with France, granted to the young republic a greater measure of respect and recognition, moderate voices in the United States might have prevailed in 1812, the war might never have taken place, and the history of North America might have been markedly different. As Britain struggled with Napoleon Bonaparte, however, North America was the last thing on British minds, rather than the first.

Off Cape Trafalgar in 1805, Horatio Nelson's Royal Navy smashes the combined French and Spanish fleets, giving Britain mastery of the sea for a century.

Napoleon's dictatorship was no more agreeable to the United States than to Great Britain, but his closing of Europe to all British trade caused Britain to retaliate by banning virtually all trade with the continent, pushing Britain and the United States closer to war.

In 1805, the British victory over the combined Spanish and French fleets at Trafalgar gave the Royal Navy indisputable command of the seas. If the British now ruled the seas, Napoleon ruled the continent of Europe, and in 1806 he handed down a decree that, command of the sea or not, any British trade with Europe was prohibited. Britain responded with Orders-in-Council forbidding all foreign trade with territory under French rule, and this particularly affected American shippers and merchants. Then, as now, the United States was a diverse society with diverse interests. New Englanders and Atlantic Coast shipowners who were doing much profitable business with Britain in food and war matériel saw little to object to in Britain's action, while men of the frontier and with a North American rather than Atlantic perspective felt the old humiliations surface at this arbitrary limitation on the American right to trade with whomever they wished.

These same men seethed with resentment when, in 1807, the Royal Navy frigate *Leopard* fired without warning on the United States frigate *Chesapeake*, inflicting casualties and then seizing several of her crew as alleged deserters from the Royal Navy. It was an act of supreme arrogance, but the American government of President Thomas Jefferson could not respond with a declaration of war, having kept American naval strength at a minimum due to a general distrust of a standing military establishment. With no military option open to him, Jefferson took recourse to an economic one, and declared an Embargo Act, which forbade *any* American trade with a foreign nation. The impact of this was felt least among the inland, frontier Americans who were Jefferson's strongest constituency; but in addition to dealing a hurtful blow at a Great Britain anxious for American goods, it also dealt a blow to those seacoast communities of the American northeast, who were making a healthy living from British trade. The New England states were for the most part suspicious of the truculent nationalism Jefferson's supporters of the west and south were demanding, and they went on finding ways to trade with Britain and its colonies, particularly through Nova Scotia, where the population was as Yankee in nature and outlook as Boston, if loyal to a different flag. As 1812 approached, there would be little sympathy for sabre-rattling in the old coastal colonies of the northeast – ironically, the seedbed of the revolution that had taken the United States out of the British family to begin with. The push to war would have to come from somewhere else.

To those in the United States who were clamouring for war, the slogan "Free Trade and Sailors' Rights" became the justifying cry. The United States could not, and should not, be bullied out of legitimate trade by the declarations of another country, they claimed, and disrespect for American citizenship was equally unacceptable. But this understandable indignation at affronts to American seaborne trade and identity masked a less noble concern, which was the territorial hunger of the burgeoning American society. The Indian and his tribes stood in the way of that hunger.

With the end of the American Revolution in 1783, a boundary had been drawn across North America, from the Atlantic to the head of the Great Lakes, which almost replicated the old divisions between New France and the Thirteen Colonies, except that British North America, unlike New France, retained none of the lands south of the Great Lakes – even though it persisted in maintaining garrisoned posts there until 1794. The frontier lands on the west side of the Appalachian chain, taking in the valleys of the Ohio and Wabash rivers south of Lake Erie and stretching as far as the southern tip of Lake Michigan, were known as the "Old Northwest." It was the home of a diverse number of Indian tribes, native to the area or recently fled there, who had remained in a virtual state of war with the American "Long Knives" and who saw in the British presence in Canada a real or potential ally in their struggle against encroaching white settlement. In a curious twist of history, the British had assumed the role of the French, whom they had conquered twenty years earlier.

Ten years after the end of the Revolution, in 1794, American troops had temporarily "resolved" the issue of Indian resistance to westward white settlement with a crushing victory over an Indian force at Fallen Timbers. The

Thomas Jefferson, *by Charles Willson Peale. Jefferson was a high-minded politician and philosopher who was not averse, however, to slave ownership. His refusal to build strong American military and naval forces, and his assurance that any conquest of Canada would be a "mere matter of marching," led the United States close to disaster.*

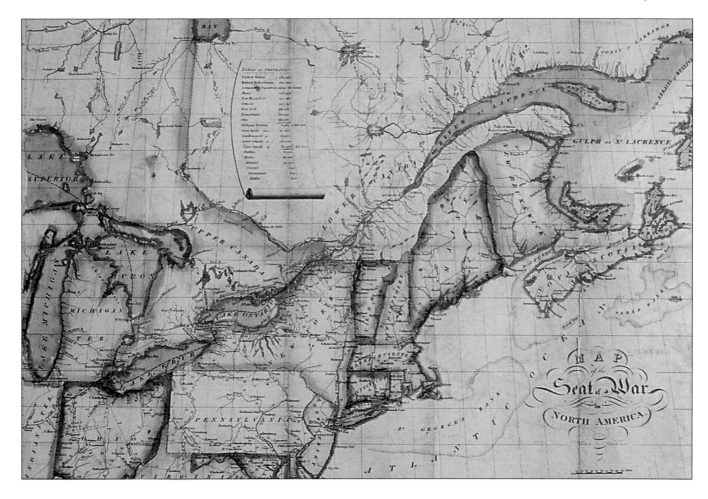

Map of Eastern North America. *The small populations of British North America in Lower Canada, Upper Canada, New Brunswick, and Nova Scotia confronted an American population fifteen times larger, and growing.*

battle took place in what was known as the Black Swamp in the valley of the Maumee River, which ran into the western end of Lake Erie. A nearby British fort shut its gates to the fleeing warriors in a lesson on the limits of British support for the Indian cause, and in the following year, 1795, a treaty of sorts, signed at the Shawnee village of Greenville, established – for the moment – a demarcation line between American lands to the east and Indian lands to the west.

The Indian land consisted roughly of the valley of the Wabash River, the northwest corner of what is now Ohio, Michigan Territory, and Indiana Territory, and stretched westward from there. In practical terms, the Wabash served as the border, but by 1811 it was being encroached upon. The men of the frontier wanted the Indian territory, as lands behind them filled up and became states, the latest being Ohio in 1803. It was in fact

A continuation of the clash between white farming settlement and Indian village culture that had commenced shortly after the seventeenth-century arrival of the Europeans on the eastern seaboard. Now, however, as the Indians resisted once more, the Americans claimed that they did so with British friendship, weapons, and supplies. A successful war with Britain, which might make it possible to take its Canadian base and end the support for the Indians, would give the Americans a free hand to smash the tribes and occupy their lands. Indiana, Michigan, and Illinois would be open to the wagons and the ploughs of American settlement, and for certain visionaries in Congress such a move could lead to the eventual claiming of all the continent.

For the British in Canada, the Indian was an ally and a useful friend. A healthy and productive Indian population meant a continuing fur

"A scene on the frontier as practised by the humane British and their worthy allies," *Philadelphia, 1812. Whatever the actual truth of British support for the Indian tribes in the Old Northwest, American popular opinion was convinced that Britain encouraged and rewarded atrocity and massacre in the warriors' resistance to American expansion.*

Young Omahaw, War Eagle, Little Missouri, and Pawnees, *by Charles Bird King. Accurate portrayals of warriors, as in this depiction of Western tribesmen, capture a dignity and resolution all the more tragic when their fate is known in retrospect.*

trade. There was also the question of protecting the remaining British territory in North America. The Napoleonic Wars had made Canada a priceless source of ship timber, pitch, tar, and other naval supplies, but its population base in the early nineteenth century was barely one-fifteenth that of the growing United States. The French along the St. Lawrence had been joined farther upriver by American loyalists, but neither they nor the small populations of Nova Scotia and New Brunswick had the numbers to meet the potential American threat. The Indian nations provided a potent ally for the Canadas' survival should an American attack materialize.

To a degree, the suspicions of the frontier Americans were accurate: British administrators and Indian agents in their far-flung posts did – as the French in Canada had done before them – become the friend of the threatened tribes. But the claimed incitement to violence and the provision of weapons laid at the British door was another matter: by 1811, Britain was stretched to the limit in her war effort against Napoleon. There were few enough arms in Canada for the militia and the thinly spread, overworked British troops. To prevent the siphoning off of needed supplies and weapons from the colonial defences, the British governors in Canada, Sir James Craig from 1807 to 1811 and Sir George Prevost after 1811, forbade Indian agents to supply muskets and ammunition to the Indian tribes, even while professing – and practising when possible – a self-interested friendship with them. This meant that the threatened Indians, facing the enmity of the approaching Americans and turning with little choice to the support of the British when the great struggle finally came for the lands of the Old Northwest, ultimately found that the friendship did not provide the weapons and the degree of military support required for a victory on the scale the Indians wanted. This situation would give the land-hungry Americans who were arguing for war the reason they needed to call for the defeat not only of the Indian nations, but also of their British supporters. It did not take much for that call to expand to an insistence that British authority be driven from the Canadas, and from North America altogether. At the same time, the inability or disinclination of Britain to provide an adequate defence for Canada, or to equip and supply its Indian allies, led Americans to think this could be accomplished.

Those Americans who believed fervently in national expansion and in sweeping aside the Indian and his British supporters were known as "War Hawks," and they found their most committed spokesman in Henry Clay of Kentucky, who declared in Congress that

Assured and determined, Henry Clay was the vociferous spokesman of the "War Hawks" and a bitter enemy of the British presence in North America.

It is absurd to suppose that we will not succeed in our enterprise against the enemy's provinces. We have the Canadas as much at our command as Great Britain has the ocean. . . . I am not for stopping at Quebec or anywhere else, but I would take the whole continent from them and ask no favours. I wish never to see peace until we do.

The War Hawks moved into influence in Washington, but found resistance from men dubious of the wisdom of any war. The Hawks countered with an assessment of British weakness that was not without some foundation, as spies reported that the strength of the thinly spread British garrisons, from Amherstburg to Fort George, Kingston, and Montreal was low; that the French Canadian population in Lower Canada – later Quebec – was unhappy and restive under the government of Sir James Craig; and that the population of Upper Canada – later Ontario – was made up largely of recent American settlers, who overbalanced the bitterly hostile Loyalists and would likely welcome rather than resist American troops. With Britain struggling interminably against Napoleon, all portents seemed ripe for action. In a stroke, the United States could crush the Indian resistance and their obstruction to the claiming of limitless new territories, and add the valuable lands of Upper Canada as well; British power in North America could be dealt a death blow, and a triumphant progress begun that would

A view of Fort George from Fort Niagara. Fort George, built on the British side of the Niagara River in 1796, after Fort Niagara reverted to American control, would be captured and held in 1813 by the Americans. Isaac Brock would leave from there to ride to his fate at Queenston in 1812, and until 1824 his body was interred in the ramparts.

create a United States reaching from Hudson Bay to Florida; and, finally, John Bull could be made to respect his cousin Jonathan.

But there were also reasons why an assumption of easy victory such as that voiced by Henry Clay would not prove true, and a good deal of this had to do with American self-deception about their military capabilities. There was no lack of courage or individual fighting ability, particularly in the populations of frontier states like Clay's Kentucky, where a pugnacious independence and the constant peril from both wilderness and hostile Indians bred accurate marksmen at ease in the wilderness and inured to brutality. The success of the Revolution had also left a belief that an armed citizenry had proven superior to regular British troops. However, this was far from the actual truth of the 1775–1783 conflict. The United States Army was small in size and boasted few senior officers who did not occupy their positions due to past heroics in the Revolution. Confronting individualistic and mercurial warriors in quick, chaotic skirmishes, followed by the burning of crops and villages, was inappropriate training, both for a supposedly friendly conquest of the Canadas, and for opposition to the British Army. Since their defeat of 1783, the British had been locked in a twenty-year struggle with the efficient troops of France, and, if the redcoats available for the defence of Canada were few in number, they were officered, for the most part, by men of experience and competence, and presented the Americans with a tough and capable enemy who would be difficult to overcome.

The War Hawks also underestimated the population of the country they wished to invade. The Canadian citizenry viewed the approaching conflict with a variety of attitudes, ranging from the implacable hatred of the Loyalists through to the indifference and uncertainty of the recently arrived Americans who now formed the largest portion of English-speaking settlers in Upper Canada and in the Eastern Townships of Lower Canada. When hostilities did eventually break out, the immediate plundering and destruction that the American troops visited on the farms and settlements of these former Americans did as much to turn them from indifference – and even welcome – to hardening resistance as would the vigorous defence of the colonies by the small British garrisons and their officers, notably Isaac Brock, commanding in Upper Canada. By the last year of the war, competent Canadian militia, speaking in accents indistinguishable from those of Vermont or Ohio, would stand in the battle line with regular British infantry against invading American forces, and would fight well. It would take some years before these men would have a clear picture of who they were, as a people, for their future nation was still too disparate in its parts to have a sense of clear identity. But the war and the depredations of the American military would make it clear to these former Americans who they were not, and in defence of their new homeland they would fight with formidable determination – not with the thrust and rapine of the Indian fighter so much as with the steady endurance of the homesteader determined not to lose what was his.

For French Canada, the practical common sense of the people would soon make it clear that the new would-be overlords were less desirable than the current ones, however the latter were disliked. As they had in 1775, the Americans misunderstood the French in thinking that Congress's exhortations on liberty would win away a majority of the people who for a hundred and fifty years had thought of the "pink-faced men of Boston," the *Bostonnais*, as the deadly enemy. In the event, French Canadians would fight with competence in the defence of the Canadas, demonstrating at Chateauguay and Lacolle as well as elsewhere that they were a people to be respected rather than assaulted.

There was an unspoken and unrecognized common feeling behind the contributions that these differing groups offered to the defence of the Canadas, which wiser heads in Washington might have expected, given their own history. In his book *The Path of Destiny*, the renowned Canadian historian Thomas Raddall explained it in 1957:

What the Americans could not see was that Canadian thought moved slowly but inevitably toward complete home rule, and home rule was not to be had by swapping a government in London for a government in Washington. The expansionist demands of the Jeffersonian party in the United States spelled domination to the Canadian as clearly as the supercilious and dictatorial manner of the British officials sent overseas to govern him. The difference was in the distance. John Bull was at least three thousand miles away. Brother Jonathan was peering right over the fence. When it came to a choice of imperialisms, the broad Atlantic lent enchantment. A few Americans recognized this. Most did not. Even after the plain disclosures of the War of 1812 the doctrine of Manifest

Destiny was still popular, and there were recurrent demands and threats and cloaked military excursions toward the Canadian border for another sixty years. But 1812 was the Canadians' year of decision. If the war showed clearly their military dependence on Britain, and set back the vague dreams of home rule for more than thirty years, it also set hard their determination to live apart from the United States.

It would be one of the great ironies of the War of 1812 that the denial of the "Manifest Destiny" of the United States to govern all of North America would come because of the actions and behaviour of those military forces launched to achieve it.

For the United States, the war brought about the rise of competent or ambitious men who would use the war to catapult them into prominence in American society. The competence of Winfield Scott would see him virtually as the pre-eminent military officer of the United States until the Civil War, and Andrew Jackson and William Henry Harrison each used a notable victory to fuel later political ambitions. However, the pressure of the war also brought an end to the careers of several men whose laurels had been earned in the distant years of the Revolution, but for whom the energy and leadership required by the war's prosecution were too great a reach. For some men, such as General William Hull, it would mean personal disaster and humiliation.

On the Canadian side, many figures remain as images on the canvas of the war, fuelling debate among historians as to their significance or irrelevance. But three stand out as demanding of a closer inspection, for they embody the aspects of the War of 1812 that make it a compelling amalgam of success and tragedy: Isaac Brock, the energetic commander of Upper Canada at the war's onset;

Andrew Jackson was a ruthless and determined frontiersman, whose accomplishments included campaigns against the southern Indians and a successful defence of New Orleans against an ill-led British attack in early 1815. He would later rise to the White House, his presidency hailed as a victory for the common man.

Tecumseh, the charismatic warrior and leader of the Indian federation allied with the British; and Sir George Prevost, the governor of the Canadas, whose policies and personal nature might have preserved Canada or risked its demise. All three men would die in the decade of the war, two during the war, and one immediately after it, as its victim. Two would die as heroes, respected by friend and foe; the third would be reviled for his hesitancy, a hero only to the daughter who adored him, his few defenders claiming he secured a deeper success his dead companions could not have achieved. It is a story of courage and folly, of hopelessness and miscalculation, and of lost opportunity.

If, as will be seen, Isaac Brock can be mourned but not pitied for having died a soldier's death, and George Prevost pitied for not having known when it was time to be a soldier, the figure of Tecumseh, the Shawnee, inspires both emotions. His death was not merely the end of one warrior's life but symbolized the death of a people's hold on a continent, and almost of their race. In life, he caused the energies of his enemies, the Americans, to be directed against him; he aroused the disparate tribes who accepted his leadership into a last, losing war; and he gave, through his own and his warriors' efforts, the necessary resistance to American power that might otherwise have enabled them to prevail over the outnumbered British. Fighting to create the idea of a final homeland, he instead made possible the future of another nation. If the denial to the Americans of the prize of Canada can be commemorated in a monument to Isaac Brock, one should also be raised to the doomed, majestic figure of Tecumseh, the Shawnee Shooting Star, whose fate was as tragic as any depicted in ancient Greek drama.

Tecumseh was an impressive and eloquent warrior and orator who had grown to manhood during the chronic Ohio border fighting of the end of the eighteenth century, becoming, in the process, a formidable fighting man, but also revealing himself as a natural leader to whom others would turn for inspiration. Gifted with a powerful and expressive speaking ability, he was also in full manhood an imposing, attractive figure, his appearance enhanced in his last years by his beautifully fitted traditional buckskin clothing, at a time when most Indian tribes of the Old Northwest had adopted the clothing of the white man. His head wrapped in silken turbans affixed

with feathers, trade silver glinting here and there, his face and features handsome and expressive, Tecumseh called forth admiration and respect from his allies and friends, but also from as resolute an adversary as Indiana's William Henry Harrison. Tecumseh roamed the western slopes of the Appalachian Mountains from north to south, but the heartland of his life was the lush river valley of the Ohio, and he had fought in the desperate efforts to resist westward American expansion that culminated in the disastrous Battle of Fallen Timbers in 1794. Tecumseh could not accept the "cession" of Indian lands that the 1795 Greenville Treaty with the Americans had arranged, and, as the century turned, he had become a trans-tribal Indian leader, speaking to tribes throughout the Ohio–Wabash area and

(Left) A conjectural portrait of the great Shawnee, based on a pencil sketch by fur trader Pierre Le Dru. No accurate portrait of Tecumseh exists, but the portraits of warriors by Charles King (page 21) suggest how impressive such a man might have been.

(Right) The defeat of the warriors by the American army at Fallen Timbers in 1794 left a bitter taste in the warriors' mouths, not only because of the defeat but because the small British garrison at Fort Miami refused to let the fleeing tribesmen take shelter within its walls.

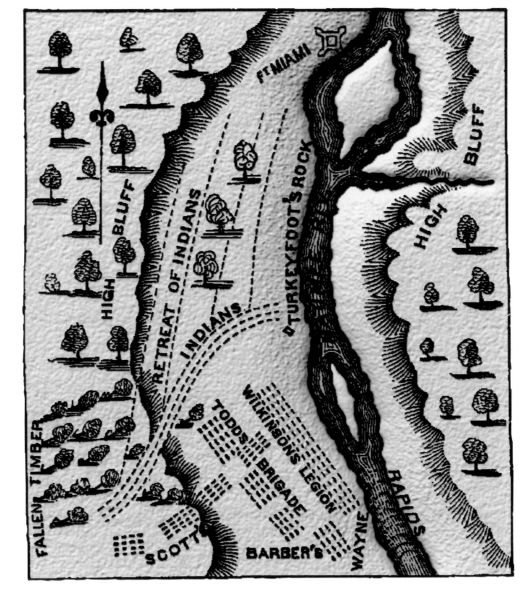

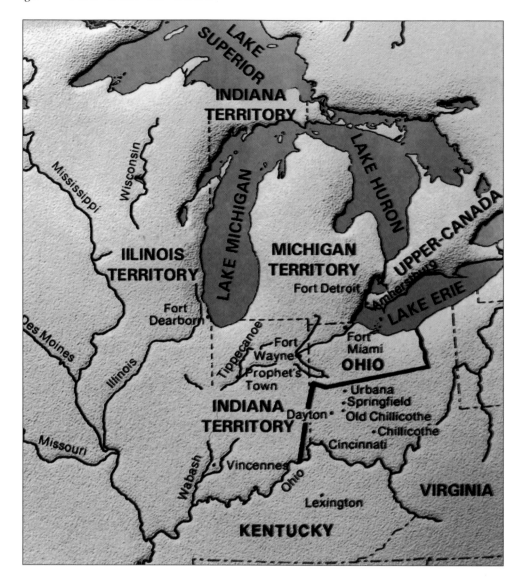

The drama of the Indian resistance in eastern North America was played to its final and tragic conclusion on the stage of the Ohio–Wabash frontier.

beyond about the need to stand together and resist the relentless lavalike encroachment of American settlement.

The tribes who heeded him were on the verge of collapse, as hunting stocks declined and old ways were forgotten or superseded. Iron and steel, cloth and flour, once oddities and luxuries, had become necessities. Riven with disease, their belief systems shaken, the tribes west of the Ohio Valley had entered into a cycle of land surrender, deprivation that led to poverty, the "sale" of lands to ease that poverty, and fresh decline and deprivation. Tecumseh moved among these despairing people with the aura of a saviour,

Known by several names, such as The Prophet and The Rattle, Lalawethika was as repelling as Tecumseh was attractive, but nonetheless gifted with a similar charisma. He claimed leadership of the desperate Indian movement in its early days, but was overshadowed by Tecumseh as the struggle with the Americans deepened.

and with an extraordinary gift of speech he pleaded passionately for Indian unity in the face of the threat posed by the "Long Knives," as they called Americans. Gradually they turned to him, overcoming mutual tribal suspicion and traditional hostility to accept him as both a military and political leader preaching a faith that was built on the repulsion of the Americans and the establishment of a common Indian homeland free of the greed and acquisitiveness of the settler society.

In this cause, he was joined by his younger brother, a man as unlike Tecumseh as it was possible to be. Lalawethika, which meant "The Rattle," was as weedy and repellent as Tecumseh was striking and attractive. Half-blind with a deformed eye, and subject to epileptic fits, Lalawethika had taken another route to leadership after escaping the disaster at Fallen Timbers, and had become a shaman, or "medicine man." Through a clever use of simple spectacle, trancelike states, and bizarre behaviour, he led people of the tribes to accept him as one touched by the Great Spirit, and in time he became known as "The Prophet." At first, it was to the strange powers of The Prophet that the remnant tribes of the Old Northwest were drawn, as he preached a compelling message, calling for a return to traditional ways as a means of ensuring Indian survival, rather than adopting the ways of the Americans. His arguments were weakened, however, by his eccentric, rather than admirable, behaviour, and his insistence that witchcraft lay behind the disease rampant in the tribal towns (which led to the persecution of women, who were the usual targets of accusations).

The influence of both men led members of a number of displaced tribes to assemble under their leadership at a new "town" on the Tippecanoe River, a tributary of the Wabash, and in the middle of the lands now coveted by the settlers. Prophet's Town, as it was known, came into being in 1808, and it was a refuge for remnants of more than half a dozen uprooted tribal groups. Tecumseh and his brother faced a capable and resolute adversary in the form of William Henry Harrison, the governor of Indiana Territory, who, in the year after the founding of Prophet's Town, convinced several petty chiefs to sign, without Tecumseh's knowledge, an agreement that turned over a two-hundred-mile swath of land drained by the Wabash–Tippecanoe system – including Prophet's Town – to white settlement.

Nothing now protected any serious Indian claim to the remaining Old Northwest, and Tecumseh turned to the British post at Amherstburg, on the Detroit River, for support. In contravention of the orders of the governor in distant Quebec, the agents of the Indian Department armed and supplied Tecumseh and his immediate followers, all the while urging the tribes to remain at peace with the Americans and pursue unity among themselves. The British aim was to retain the Indians as an intact force until the actual moment when they might be needed in conflict with the Americans, rather than tempting the Long Knives to destroy them too soon.

This fact was not lost on the ambitious and perceptive Harrison, who now forced the issue while Tecumseh was absent in the south promoting Indian unity. In 1811, Harrison struck at the assembled tribes on the Tippecanoe, defeating the warriors under Lalawethika and abruptly ending his influence, as well as burning Prophet's Town to the ground. For an aghast Tecumseh, there was now no recourse; to survive against

The uneven Battle of Tippecanoe, on November 6, 1811, shattered the Prophet's reputation as an effective leader of the warriors, and convinced Tecumseh that all-out war with the Americans was inevitable.

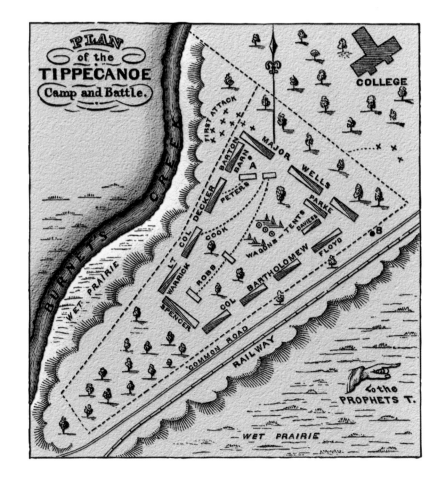

the relentless American pressure, he had to commit to the British alliance in the inner knowledge that his ancestral lands were lost. Perhaps, with a formal war between Britain and the United States, there would be a chance to secure British support for a new – final – Indian homeland. It was this chance Tecumseh now pursued, knowing there was no other. In the event, he would die without seeing the dream materialize, but through his efforts and those of his warriors, he earned a kind of bittersweet posthumous victory: the warriors' efforts in large part denied the whole continent to Harrison and the War Hawks, but the homeland they helped create was not the Indian refuge of their dreams. It was the modern nation of Canada.

This graphic portrayal of the crisis of the Tippecanoe struggle, painted many years later by an unknown artist, is misleading in its depiction of the warriors. Tribes of the Old Northwest had by 1811 largely adopted European clothing, leading Tecumseh to stand out dramatically in his hand-sewn buckskins, and warriors were unlikeley to have fought semi-naked or wearing large feather bonnets like the figure in the foreground.

If Tecumseh was a towering figure cast in heroic proportions, the British officer responsible for the defences of Upper Canada, Major General Isaac Brock, was a match for him in everything, from an impressive appearance to the fighting spirit that the unequal struggle of 1812–1814 so required. Like the Shawnee, Brock was attractive and charismatic, tall for the age and strongly built. He was a Channel Islander who had served in the British Army from an early age and had come to Canada first in 1802, returning only briefly to England. In 1811, the year of Tippecanoe, he had not only been made military commander in Upper Canada but had taken over the civil government as well, when the incumbent governor, Francis Gore, went on leave to England for health reasons.

Brock was all too aware of the small and thinly spread defences he would be able to mount against the building American threat, and how the American origins of much of the Canadian population made the problem of defending Upper Canada even greater.

An active, energetic man who read the Classics, Brock saw himself and any coming struggle in Homeric terms, as the pitting of a Greek hero against enormous odds in a struggle worthy of valiant effort. It was characteristic of him that he determined to adopt an aggressive defence of his territory rather than sheltering behind the claim of insufficient men or supplies. *Audace, toujours l'audace* – "Audacity, always audacity" – might well have been his motto, for he intended in any fighting with the Americans to carry the war to them, hoping by initiative and spirit to make up for lack of trained soldiers. It would also demonstrate to the citizenry that a vigorous defence would be in place, to which they could give allegiance. It was an attitude that led Tecumseh to recognize him as a kindred spirit when the men finally met.

But Brock was human, and, if cast as Achilles, had his heel of weakness. In his case it was an inability to restrain his audacity in favour of prudence, and he would die characteristically leading an infantry charge against the American position at Queenston Heights, in the first year of the war. Brock's conviction that vigorous defence might overcome his lack of resources was astute in the larger sense; he was less able to realize that his value to a cause required him to live for it, rather than die. Tecumseh would die as he might have wished, in a final battle with the victorious American troops, the hated frontier men who had smashed his dreams; Brock would die needlessly when his dream of an unconquered Canada was still real – and needed him alive to keep it so. No death of fine men, in any age, can be celebrated, but these deaths suggested larger tragedies. What would the cause of the Indian in North America, in Canada, during the unfolding nineteenth century have been if Tecumseh had lived to be its eloquent spokesman? And what would have been the outcome for Britain and for Canada if Brock had lived, and not left the defence of the colonies in hands that were never as capable as his? Nowhere is the waste of war more evident than in this double loss, even if neither question is answerable. The monument that marks where Brock fell near Queenston is not matched by one for his warrior brother: Tecumseh lies in an unknown country grave, its

(Left) Capable, audacious, and beloved by his men, Isaac Brock distrusted the largely American civilian population of Upper Canada and worried about the small numbers of his troops. He would die bravely, if unwisely, and his initiative, along with the warriors' alliance, helped Canada hold out in the early days of the war.

whereabouts lost to time. Perhaps the towering pillar to Brock may be seen as a monument to what both men might have become, had not war taken them from the people – and the country – who needed them.

To cast Brock and Tecumseh as classical heroes is to recognize in them a certain simplicity, to see them, whether incorrectly or not, as transparent in their intentions, in their commitment to forthright and vigorous action.

The third major figure in the War of 1812 story for Canada, Sir George Prevost, the Governor General of the Canadas, is anything but transparent in character, and in many respects he plays an even more tragic role in the drama than did either Brock or Tecumseh. For the latter two, the answer lay in action; for Prevost, the answer lay in the avoidance of action, in dodging the climactic confrontation in which all is gambled, and won – or lost. Yet in Prevost's case avoidance destroyed him as surely as action destroyed Brock and Tecumseh. Canada might have survived because of him, or in spite of him. The debate about which view is correct still engrosses historians and leaves his appropriate place in history unclear to this day.

Sir George Prevost was a cautious and careful man. His social skills put him at ease in a drawing room, but he was hesitant to fight when the situation called for it. His timidity may have risked rather than saved Canada – the debate continues – but his career would end in ruins.

Sir George Prevost was a career British officer of Swiss descent who had been appointed to the senior post in the Canadas partly because of his fluency in French. He had served capably, if not with particular distinction, in the West Indies, and after a defence of the island of Dominica against a short-lived French attack in 1805, he had been knighted. When he came to Canada he was soon able to establish better relations with the French population than had the crusty Sir James Craig before him. He was fair-complexioned and youthful-looking, with a hesitant cast to his expression and a tendency to appear too small for his clothes. Yet he was sociable and accommodating, and his apparent qualities of prudence and conciliation seemed well suited for his post in Canada. The defensive, husbanding manner that had served him to date might have appeared ideal to the British government that appointed him. From their distant position in London, preoccupied with the European war, the gentlemen of His Britannic Majesty's government might have decided that a remote and penniless colony with a tiny garrison needed a cautious and conserving sort of man at its helm. And that Prevost was. His daughter, Anne, however, had a premonition that his appointment to Canada would not be a happy one:

View of Quebec City, 1838, *by Richard Coke Smith. The fortified citadel, shown in this later view, was Sir George Prevost's headquarters, and he was prepared to abandon all of Canada to the Americans to hold it.*

It is strange but most true, that I felt a presentiment that my prosperity was on its wane, and that unhappiness awaited me, though I had no reason whatever to anticipate such a change at the time. My Father was going to take possession of an appointment which brought him a greater degree of influence and honour, – it was a mark of his Prince's confidence in his talents – yet this day my naturally cheerful spirits were subdued, and I could see nothing before me but gloom.

– Journal of Anne Prevost, later addition to entry for August 25, 1811

Anne Prevost's diary gives glimpses of a young girl leading the privileged life of a governor's daughter, yet is full of anguish as her father's career disintegrated. The war would take from her not only her father, but also a suitor with whom she may have been in love.

As the War Hawks achieved their ascendancy in Washington, Prevost had little enough in the way of forces stretched up the thousand-mile river-and-lake corridor to Montreal, Kingston, the mouth of the Niagara and Detroit rivers, and the remote island of St. Joseph at the head of Lake Huron. Besides his few thousand regular British soldiery – fewer than five thousand from Nova Scotia to St. Joseph Island – he had militias of uncertain loyalty and quality in Upper and Lower Canada, a small naval force of the army's "Provincial Marine" on Lake Ontario, some naval presence on Lake Erie and on the lakes above, a regiment of aged veterans, and three regiments enlisted largely from among the Canadians: the Canadian Voltigeurs, the Glengarry Light Infantry, and the Canadian Fencible Regiment. The United States was capable, on paper, of overmatching this entire force with the militia of Kentucky alone, and Prevost's approach was always to restrain Brock and other attack-minded officers while husbanding resources at minimal risk. He was not the first to command a remote position and be fearful of the wrong move that would lose everything, and he made it clear to the impetuous Brock that he wanted no risking of Crown resources in a war he hoped would soon go away. In his defence, it must be remembered that he was subordinate to officials who did not wish to be disturbed by the Canadian problem. Perhaps his cautious policy was the only one conceivable to a governor with so vast and vulnerable an area to defend – and so little to defend it with.

By 1812 the difficulties facing American shipping and sailors at the hands of the British was causing an uproar in Congress, as was news of the struggle on the Ohio–Wabash watershed with the Indians under Tecumseh. The War Hawks had found eloquent spokesmen in men like Henry Clay, John C. Calhoun, and Joseph Desha of Kentucky, who saw in Britain's presence on the continent the impediment that would have to be smashed aside if the new western lands were to be taken, the Indians dealt with, and the destiny of the United States fulfilled. Britain in North America was the cause of the troubles, said Desha, and "you must remove the cause if you expect to perform the cure." These men had come into Congress in the elections of 1810, and were joined by other hawkish advocates of war such as Peter B. Porter of New York, and John Harpen of New Hampshire, who went against the anti-war sentiment of his fellow New Englanders. Clay, the practical leader of the movement, was a Kentuckian who represented a frontier

population that had to deal with ruthless Indian resistance, and the assumed British support for it. The War Hawks have been portrayed as determined young men, impatient with the moderate Federalists, who to them were old Revolutionary War leaders in whose hands power still lay. They wanted the Indian lands, they wanted the British out of North America, and they wanted British respect elsewhere. Finally they would succeed in pushing President James Madison into a declaration of war he would have preferred not to make.

Madison's caution was appropriate. Great Britain was the world's foremost naval power, had an equally competent army, and would be in no

The Old House of Representatives, by Samuel F. B. Morse. This later portrayal pictures the floor of Congress, where the War Hawks' exhortations towards war with Britain gradually won the day over more moderate voices, particularly those from New England.

John C. Calhoun was among the most vocal of the War Hawks, seeing the British and Indian alliance as an impediment to American growth that had to be swept aside.

John Randolph of Virginia saw little merit in the war, ascribing its cause less to British bullying than to "our own thirst for territory, our own want of moderation."

mood to be irritated while fighting Napoleon. In addition, if there were War Hawks insisting on war, there were also moderate voices, like that of John Randolph of Virginia, who saw little glory and much land-grabbing in the process. In New England particularly, historic, personal, and economic ties with Britain and the colonies of Nova Scotia and New Brunswick made the westerners' war pressure so unpopular that, when war did come, an active and serious secessionist movement arose that threatened to split apart the United States. By 1811, however, the War Hawks were in full cry in Congress. Clay had become Speaker of the House of Representatives and Porter head of the House Committee on Foreign Affairs. In vain did John Randolph argue that British bullying was less the cause for war than "our own thirst for territory, our own want of moderation." On the eve of war, some conciliatory moves by the British government were learned of too late to stay James Madison's hand on June 18, 1812, as he signed the declaration of war between the United States of America and Great Britain. The United States, however, entered into the conflict poorly prepared for war, both against the battle-hardened and huge Royal Navy – although, individually, American ships were superb – and against the tiny populations of Upper and Lower Canada and their small-but-capable garrisons. Former President Thomas Jefferson's distrust of a standing military meant that Madison's government would have to rely greatly on militia forces. But then, Jefferson had assured the nation that the conquest of the Canadas would be "a mere matter of marching."

The news of the formal declaration of war arrived in Canada by roundabout means, Brock learning of it through contact with an employee of New York fur trader John Jacob Astor, and Prevost by similar means. It was an inauspicious beginning, and the Canadas were in real peril. To the young Anne Prevost, however, all portents were good, and her earlier gloom dispelled:

> I saw nothing before me but my Father's honour and glory. Although
> I knew how small a force we had to defend the Canadas, such was my
> confidence in his talents and fortune, that I did not feel the slightest
> apprehension of any reverse. I thought those abominable Yankees

James Madison's decision to declare war on Great Britain, and press on with it despite conciliatory British moves, would bring military disaster, humiliation, and near bankruptcy to the United States.

deserved a good drubbing for having dared to think of going to war with England, and surely there was no harm in rejoicing that the War had happened during my Father's administration, because I thought he was the person best calculated to inflict on the Yankees the punishment they deserved. Stars and Ribbons glittered in perspective.

– Journal of Anne Prevost, later addition to entry for June 25, 1812

William Eustis was a medical doctor who brought little knowledge or administrative ability to the demanding position of secretary of war, and failed to resolve the problem of incompetent army leadership early in the conflict.

Now that war had been declared, the United States had to set about waging it. A principal problem, as already mentioned, was lack of military leadership, the main resource being men who had served during the distant Revolution, and at relatively junior rank. Since then they had been seasoned only with Indian skirmishes. To add to the American woes, neither the secretary of war, Dr. William Eustis, nor the secretary of the navy, Paul Hamilton, brought any real competence to their understaffed offices. They were nonetheless expected to get on with the task. Eustis assigned a

(Above left) Commander of the campaign against Canada in the first part of the war, Revolutionary War veteran Henry Dearborn was unable to capitalize on opportunities won for the United States by more competent juniors.

(Above right) William Hull would surrender his superior force at Detroit to Brock and Tecumseh without a struggle. His defeat, and the depredations of his troops, did much to strengthen Canadian resistance to the Americans.

Revolutionary War veteran, Henry Dearborn, to head the army and its operations against Canada, and a slate of brigadier generals of varying abilities was appointed. The governor of Michigan Territory, William Hull, was handed a generalcy and the first opportunity to demonstrate that the conquest of the Canadas would be simply a marching exercise.

For Isaac Brock, the impending hostilities meant it was time to play the Indian card, to call on the many tribes in the Great Lakes region to rally with the British against the Long Knives, and thus redress the imbalance in the defences. Tecumseh and his warriors were more than willing to fight – only wanting a demonstration that the British were equally committed – and the British policy of encouraging restraint and unity in the western tribes meant that a capable fighting force was indeed there. Britain's old allies, the Iroquois, who still remembered their defeat in the American Revolution and the desolation of the Mohawk Valley, determined for the moment to observe

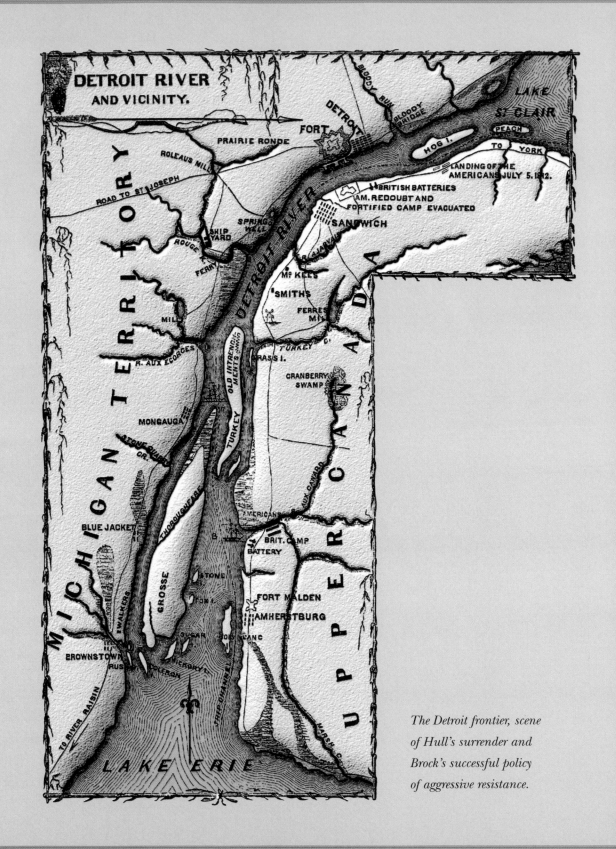

The Detroit frontier, scene of Hull's surrender and Brock's successful policy of aggressive resistance.

neutrality, but there was still a sufficient Indian force available to Brock to do what he knew he must: carry the war to the United States before the Americans carried it to the Canadas.

William Hull's intentions to march an army against Canada at the Detroit frontier became common knowledge very quickly after Hull had assembled a heterogenous force of regular soldiery and of militia in Ohio, and when he led that force out of camp on June 12, 1812, a week before the actual declaration of war, Brock knew what was afoot. That general knowledge became quite specific when, on July 2, the small American schooner *Cuyahoga* made its way into the Detroit River from Lake Erie, bound for Fort Detroit. It was halted by the British guns of Fort Malden, at Amherstburg, and when a British boarding party of the Provincial Marine clambered aboard they found Hull's campaign baggage and documents, the latter outlining not only the nature of his force, but his detailed war plans. Hull had gambled that word of war's declaration would not reach Fort Malden before the *Cuyahoga* had sailed peacefully on to Fort Detroit. The dilemma facing the British was what to do with this intelligence, given the tiny size of their forces.

The capture of the Cuyahoga *off Fort Malden placed William Hull's plans in the hands of the British, but also alerted Brock to Hull's hesitation and worry.*

Hull himself arrived at Fort Detroit uneventfully on July 5, 1812, with a force of some 2,500 men. His role, and that of another simultaneous attack to be launched somehow on the Niagara frontier, was not only to invade but in doing so to draw British attention away from the St. Lawrence River Valley, where a principal American attack up the Champlain Valley route would secure the Canadas for Congress in one season. Downriver at Fort Malden, it seemed to that tiny British garrison that Hull was capable of doing whatever he wished. There were but 150 regular infantry, some 300 untried militia, and 150 warriors under Tecumseh available to resist whatever the Americans had planned.

Hull soon demonstrated he was not a man of lightning action, however. It took a full week of preparation before he crossed the Detroit River on July 12, landing at Sandwich, where Windsor now stands. Hull made no move downriver towards Fort Malden, instead spending his time drafting a proclamation to the inhabitants of Canada that intoned, "The United States offers you Peace, Liberty, and Security. Your choice is between these and War, Slavery, and Destruction." Unfortunately, the initial contact of the Canadian civil population with the peace, liberty, and security of the United States was a subsequent swath of plunder and looting that Hull's troops inflicted on peaceful settlements as far as sixty miles up the Thames River. If inclined earlier, because of sentiment or ancestry, to welcome the American forces, the inhabitants, for the most part, now turned in dismay and finally anger against them. It was the first, and one of the most significant, blunders of the American execution of the war, turning what might well have been a receptive populace into an implacably hostile one, and ensuring that the "mere matter of marching" would become a bloody and bitter struggle full of waste and savagery.

While Fort Malden looked anxiously to its powder and wondered why Hull's force had not swept down on it, news arrived of a British victory far to the north. Brock had been urged by Prevost to avoid attacking the Americans, but had nonetheless told the British commander of the small post on St. Joseph Island, at the head of Lake Huron, to act as his judgement directed. The commander, Captain Charles Roberts, read between the lines and decided to pounce on the nearby American post of Fort Mackinac, on Mackinac Island. Roberts felt certain the Americans there had not heard of the declaration of war, and the taking of the American

Osage Scalp Dance by John Mix Stanley. The intimidating physical power of the Indian warrior was a source of dread for the frontier American of the early nineteenth century. British policy throughout the war deliberately played upon the American fear of the warrior as a means of gaining military advantage, as Isaac Brock demonstrated at Detroit.

post would dramatically encourage the western tribes to rally to the British cause. Roberts embarked a small party of the 10th Foot (Royal Veterans), and with four hundred Indians alongside in canoes, he sailed over in the Northwest Company's fur-trading vessel *Caledonia* to Mackinac Island. Landing on its one practical beach on the northwest side, Roberts positioned a small gun on a rise overlooking the fort and called on the American garrison to surrender. The Americans did so, and in a bloodless stroke Roberts had taken a key post in the northwest, one that dominated the passage into Lake Michigan. He had also given the western Indians tangible proof that the redcoats were, at last, prepared to fight. Tecumseh, at Fort Malden, found warriors streaming south to join him, and within several weeks had not 150 warriors, but 600.

If the news was electrifying for Tecumseh and the British at Fort Malden, it was a catastrophe for Hull, "opening the hive," as he put it, of Indian participation in the war as they flocked to Tecumseh's side. Fear of the Indian warrior would remain the Achilles heel of the American military throughout the War of 1812 – and with good reason. The legacy of slaughter and bitter hostility which had grown between the United States and the

Indian arose in part from the natural clash of a hunting, partly agricultural, society with an encroaching one that had irreconcilable concepts of land ownership, but also from the pattern of mutual atrocity they had visited upon one another since the earliest days of the European settlement of North America. Now, the inability of American governments to provide a survival option for the Indian and his society, their repeated breaking of treaty agreements, and their expulsion of tribe after tribe from desired lands had closed the book on reconciliation with the Indian, with the exception of pacified tribes such as the Cherokee, who tried to live as the Americans urged them to, in the white way in settled farming towns. (The Cherokee would learn, a quarter-century later, that living in the white way would not protect them.) For Tecumseh's warriors, the frontier American was almost inevitably an enemy to be fought to the death, without mercy, and it was a racial as well as a cultural enmity which could end only with the

Indian Encampment on Lake Huron, *by Paul Kane. Large encampments of warriors and their families such as this sprang up around Fort Malden and other British posts, as different tribes rallied to Tecumseh's call.*

defeat or death of the opponent: a species of tribal war. American prisoners could expect little mercy if taken alive, unless adoption saved them, and Brock and other British commanders used this fear to their benefit. Now, that particular fear hung over William Hull, immobile in his encampment, while his mounted troops spread a legacy of waste and resentment in the countryside and the tiny garrison at Fort Malden watched and waited.

For Isaac Brock, in the little Upper Canadian capital at York – the "muddy York" that someday would become Toronto – the threat of Hull's force looming over Fort Malden and the Detroit frontier was compounded by an equal threat from the growing American troop strength just across the Niagara River. To lose the Niagara frontier would be to lose all of Upper Canada west of there; there would be no way to supply and protect it effectively, since access to Lake Erie would be lost. But Brock gambled that there was time to deal with the Niagara threat, and determined that a strike of some kind against Hull was needed immediately. On August 5, 1812, Brock crossed from York to Burlington Bay and overland to the shores of Lake Erie, where he and three hundred militia embarked in a mixed flotilla for Amherstburg. He paused only to speak to the Council of the Mohawks on the Grand River in an unsuccessful attempt to stir them from their cautious neutrality, and then pressed on in a risky, rain-sodden voyage, arriving at Fort Malden on the night of August 13. There he found that a shift of momentum had taken place, from the American engine of war to the British.

York Barracks, 1804. York (present-day Toronto) and its modest defences served as Isaac Brock's headquarters as well as the capital of Upper Canada. The small community lay at the beginning of the cartway leading north towards Georgian Bay and Lake Simcoe, and on the road from Kingston to the Niagara Peninsula, but it was vulnerable to attack from American vessels on Lake Ontario.

Hull had remained in his position on the Canadian shore, as if frozen in indecision. Fort Malden was still unthreatened, save for some light skirmishing. But Tecumseh's warriors had intercepted messengers from Detroit, and learned that a needed supply column under Captain Henry Brush was making its way north from western Ohio to Hull, and that Hull was sending out an escort force under Major Thomas Van Horne to meet it. Henry Procter, the British commander at Fort Malden, sent out some of Tecumseh's warriors and a party of infantry and militia to prepare an ambush on the American side of the river. Near Brownstown, south of Detroit, this party, the warriors in the forefront of the fighting, surprised and routed Van Horne's escort on August 5. Hull's mail bags were found and turned over to Procter, revealing the state of Hull's force – and Hull's increasing fear.

With Van Horne's defeat and the arrival of the news from Fort Mackinac, Hull's aggressive spirit vanished altogether, and on August 11 he ordered his army back across the river to Fort Detroit, having occupied Canadian soil for a month and done little but irritate the civilian population. Two days earlier, in a confused little engagement at Maguaga, just north of Brownstown, a British–Indian force with some inexperienced men had fired on itself

View of Detroit, 1794, from the south. The Canadian shore is to the right of the picture.

as much as the enemy, but managed to repulse a second force sent out by Hull to try and reach Brush's supply column, which was now halted on the Maumee River and uncertain what to do. Hull settled deeper into the shelter of Fort Detroit and his own gloom, his ardour for invasion and conquest now gone, largely due to Indian initiative and Procter's energy. Two days after Hull evacuated Canada, Brock arrived with his boat-weary militia to find not a besieged post, but an enemy gone to ground in a fortification, having given up the field to a smaller opponent. The British were now free to plan how to get at him.

It was at this point that Brock and Tecumseh met, in a lamplit room at Fort Malden, and it was said that both men instantly liked and respected one another. The two figures, one tall and powerfully built, in the red uniform coat of the British Army, the other just as impressive in buckskin and trade silver, represented the best of the joint hopes of the Indians and the defenders of Canada. In little more than a year, both would be dead. But for the moment, the tide of conflict had turned in their favour. Brock was presented with the documents captured from the *Cuyahoga* and a summary of events to date, and a picture emerged of Hull as a frightened and confused man, distrusted by his own officers and soldiery, convinced that he was surrounded by limitless hordes of warriors backed by a large and growing British garrison at Fort Malden. Brock characteristically determined to attack him before more astute or courageous spirits took command of the American force. "Ho! This is a man!" Tecumseh is said to have exulted.

It was a decision fraught with risk. Hull still had between two and three thousand capable infantry and cavalry, backed by field guns, and against his fortified position Brock could muster only some three hundred redcoats, four hundred untried militiamen, and the six hundred warriors of Tecumseh. He had in addition some artillery, and the guns of the Provincial Marine vessel *Queen Charlotte*, which was based at Amherstburg. If Brock's officers were uncertain as to the wisdom of attacking a fortified force twice their size, however, Tecumseh's enthusiasm knew no bounds. It took two days to move the little force up to Sandwich, opposite Fort Detroit, and Brock began by sending two aides over with a flag of truce and a call to Hull to surrender, citing the difficulty of controlling the Indians if the assault took place. Hull refused, and Brock's small battery of guns, the guns of the *Queen Charlotte*, and the American guns in Fort Detroit began to batter

Bombardment of Detroit, August 1812 –
British Ships Off Sandwich. *The Provincial
Marine's most powerful vessel on the Detroit
frontier,* Queen Charlotte, *lent her guns to
the bombardment of Fort Detroit.*

at one another. That night, Tecumseh took warriors across the river and ensured that a landing place was clear.

The morning of August 16 dawned, and with it came Brock and every man he could clothe and arm, along with a small battery of guns. They clambered ashore from their boats and formed up in column on the rutted Ohio roadway, ready to march north towards the fort, into which shells and round shot were falling. With the warriors in the flanking forests, the little force trudged up the roadway, Tecumseh and Brock riding together at its head.

In Fort Detroit, Hull's officers did not lack courage, and were in a lather of frustration, urging Hull to take offensive action, to attack the Sandwich batteries, or to sally out with the main body and defeat Brock's troops before the fort. But Hull was already a beaten man. Shells were bursting inside the walls, and his family was with him. Brock's militia, although made up of farm men barely able to march together in a line, were clothed largely in used red uniform coats, castoffs of the regulars, and this gave Brock's force – now arrayed before the fort in three columns, to seem larger – the look of an impressive body of infantry. Meanwhile, Tecumseh's warriors in the flanking woods were deliberately raising such a din of frightening yells and cries that to the watching defenders it seemed the forest was alive with them. Brock advanced, his eyes on the earthen and log walls ahead, watching for a sign his gamble had worked. And then, before a single musket shot was fired, a white flag rose up the fort's flagstaff. The horror of an Indian massacre had overcome Hull, and he gave up without a struggle, to the astounded dismay of his officers.

Having demonstrated at last to Tecumseh and the warriors that they would fight, the British also gained in material goods by the victory. The fort contained many guns, stores, and horses, and in addition to those prizes there was the brig *Adams*, which had recently been built, and which now – renamed – joined the *Queen Charlotte* in the Lake Erie resources of the Provincial Marine as the *Detroit*. For the captured American troops, the terms of surrender were not as punitive as they might have been if the battle had occurred later in the war, when bitterness over the burning and looting of villages, and mutual massacre, became a factor. The professional soldiery, including a despondent Hull and his officers, began a tedious voyage to Quebec, while the members of the militia were simply sent off home on their promise not to serve again in the war. It was a stunning victory, in which Brock's audacity, counterbalancing his few resources, had proven appropriate. The news of the capture of Detroit and Mackinac further hardened the support of the Canadian civil population, even as it burst upon a shocked Congress with the impact of one of *Queen Charlotte*'s rounds.

While Brock was displaying the value of aggressive thinking, and had the good fortune to do so against someone not willing to fight him, Sir George Prevost at Quebec was trying to find ways of either limiting the war or avoiding it completely. In this he received help from the British government, which had repealed several offensive Orders-in-Council against American trade on July 23, 1812, and had sent out notification of that to Prevost, along with a directive to seek some kind of armistice with the Americans. The American plan for winning the war had remained relatively simple: Henry Dearborn, now "First Major General" of the United States Army, had established his headquarters at Albany, New York. While he gathered a force in the Lake Champlain Valley, he expected that William Hull would strike over the Detroit frontier, his offensive matched by a similar American thrust across the Niagara River to be commanded by Stephen Van Rensselaer. The threat of these two assaults would cause Prevost to weaken the defences of Quebec and Lower Canada by sending troops west, and at that moment Dearborn would strike with his force for Montreal and Quebec up the classic Champlain–Richelieu invasion route.

Now Dearborn at Albany received the offer of armistice from Prevost, and accepted it on August 6, albeit pending approval from Washington.

Prevost lost no time in directing Brock, partway through an aggressive strategy of action which had proven remarkably successful at Detroit, to act only out of defensive necessity. Brock's actions were well on the way to providing so many obstacles for the Americans to overcome that the defence of the Canadas would have been that much more secure. Now, in a stroke, his hands were tied.

Henry Procter at Fort Malden not only had Fort Detroit in his possession, but he had put together a mixed little force of redcoats and Indians under Captain Adam Muir, who had fought competently in the ambush of Van Horne's force, and had sent them off to attack Fort Wayne, in Indiana

Territory southwest of Lake Erie. Now, Muir too was halted, allowing the tiny garrison of Fort Wayne to be reinforced and a new American army in the Old Northwest to be assembled under the career soldier General James Winchester. Muir retired to Fort Malden, an opportunity lost, and the incredulous Indian warriors began to desert, memories of the Fallen Timbers disaster of 1794 and of British indifference replacing the enthusiasm Brock's actions had produced.

Behind the retirement, the Americans had time to regroup and rearm, and now Winchester moved north in pursuit of Muir with several thousand infantry, while behind him the governor of Indiana Territory and newly minted general William Henry Harrison began the assembly of a militia-based fighting force from the frontier states that would move north in overwhelming force. When, on August 29, 1812, Washington informed Dearborn that the armistice was ended, Prevost's limitations on Brock had thrown away the gains won in the west, and had prevented him from mounting a Detroit-style assault on Van Rensselaer's forces massing on the Niagara River frontier. More ominously, it had done incalculable harm to the trusting alliance with Tecumseh and his warriors, which had been won by Brock's firmness and initiative. Prevost may well have been responding

The Amherstburg and Detroit Rivers, 1813. *Amherstburg and Fort Malden are to the right in this scene, which looks north. Bois Blanc Island is visible on the left.*

to clear directives from a remote and self-preoccupied British government, not to mention his own cautious convictions, but he had effectively taken away the weapon the defence of the Canadas had required in the face of overwhelming American numerical strength: boldness and initiative. Part of Prevost's duty as the commander in the field was to inform the British government when its policies were wrong, and more likely to do harm than good. Now he had given the United States time to recover, without penalty, from an initial series of reverses that, if exploited by aggressive strategy, might have convinced a fractious Congress that the war was too costly – and unwinnable. That was not now the case.

If Congress was given a rude shock with the double disasters of Mackinac and Detroit, and the sobering reality that the British redcoat and his Indian ally were going to be a tough nut to crack, whatever the selective memories of the Revolution, the small-but-able United States Navy was providing some welcome evidence of American competence elsewhere. President Jefferson's distrust of a standing military had kept the republic's naval force small. But the sea-going traditions of America were strong, and capable men manned well-designed and well-built ships – if few – particularly a class of "super frigate" that included the *Constitution*, 44 guns. On August 19, 1812, three days after Hull's surrender, *Constitution* met the British frigate *Guerrière*, 38 guns, and defeated her soundly, beginning a series of single-ship victories against the Royal Navy that did much to assuage the humiliations of the past. It also made clear to the Royal Navy that, however complacent it had become about its tradition of naval victories over the French and Spanish, it had a new foe that – man for man and ship for ship – was as good as it was, and frequently better. The huge size of the Royal Navy and its ability to blockade the American coast at will could not detract from the gallant record that would be established by the United States Navy in the war at sea, and at key moments in the naval war on the Great Lakes as well.

Prevost's application of the armistice also limited the abilities of the small British naval flotillas on the lakes to support Brock. The Provincial Marine on Lake Ontario and Lake Erie, though manned by men with little training for war, had been able to make its presence known, both in assisting Brock in the reduction of Fort Detroit and in delivering troops and supplies to the Niagara-frontier forces. The Marine's squadron at Kingston, Ontario,

USS Constitution *batters HMS* Guerrière *into submission, August 19, 1812. The competence and fighting ability of the small United States Navy was a rude shock to the Royal Navy, which had grown accustomed to victory against the French and Spanish.*

consisted of four major vessels, of which the most effective was the small, ship-rigged frigate of some twenty guns, *Royal George.*

Master Commandant Hugh Earl, in *Royal George*, served as commodore of the squadron, and whether at the urging of Brock or of his own officers, Earl had taken the inexperienced little force across the eastern end of Lake Ontario on July 19, towards the small American naval post at Sackets Harbor, New York. Here, Lieutenant Melancthon Woolsey, USN, had an even smaller force, centred on the brig *Oneida.* On Earl's approach, Woolsey stoutly defended his anchored vessels and the harbour, with the assistance of shore batteries, and after a lacklustre effort Earl sailed off, with only some damage inflicted by Woolsey's guns to show for the day's enterprise. Woolsey continued to show a dash and competence – which contrasted painfully with the performance of the Provincial Marine – a week or so later, when he sent off the schooner *Julia* to intercept two Provincial Marine vessels, *Moira* and *Gloucester*, which were sailing down the St. Lawrence River to Ogdensburg, New York, in order to capture some American lake schooners sheltering there. The *Julia* came upon the two British schooners, and fought so tenaciously that the latter gave up the effort, and *Julia* and the schooners later returned upriver to Lake Ontario, and Sackets Harbor, in triumph under the cover of the Prevost–Dearborn armistice.

The Provincial Marine's only moment of real success came on October 1, 1812, when the *Royal George* anchored in Lake Ontario off the mouth of the Genesee River, and Earl captured two vessels at the village of Charlotte, New York, near present-day Rochester. Bottled up on their seacoasts by the British blockade, the United States Navy was preparing to send more able men and supplies to the Great Lakes, and the incapacity of the transport-oriented Provincial Marine to carry the war to a temporarily weaker enemy

Melancthon Woolsey distinguished himself early in the war by a spirited defence of Sackets Harbor against an attack by the Provincial Marine squadron from Kingston, and remained one of Isaac Chauncey's better officers.

Kingston, the former French post of Cataraqui, became the base of Sir James Lucas Yeo's Lake Ontario Squadron of the Royal Navy in 1813. Situated at the point where Lake Ontario empties into the St. Lawrence, it was the key post for the control of Upper Canada, but the Americans never threatened its considerable defences.

British Attack on Sackets Harbor on Lake Ontario, 1812. *Twice during the war, British vessels based at Kingston threatened the United States Navy base at Sackets Harbor. The first attack was repulsed by Woolsey; the second would be called off by Sir George Prevost just as success was within reach of a British landing party. Here, British vessels work up into the bay towards Sackets Harbor with the benefit of a southerly wind.*

was an ominous sign of what the future would hold unless a parallel to the zeal and determination of a Brock was brought to the looming contest for the lakes and for the vital water-supply routes to Upper Canada.

Sir George Prevost's apparent personal unwillingness to do more than minimally fight the war seems to have hinged on his sense of being limited by the resources available to him. Certainly his family felt him to be a determined defender of the colony:

> On the arrival of the news of the War, my Mother had some thought of going to England with her children. Had Sir James Craig's plan of defence been pursued Quebec would inevitably have soon been surrounded by a besieging army, for he did not intend to offer any opposition until the Enemy were before the walls of Quebec. My Father had resolved to adopt a much bolder plan: he determined to throw his forces forward and to defend his immense frontier of nearly a thousand miles "inch by inch."
>
> – *Journal of Anne Prevost, later addition to entry for July 23, 1812*

The defence of Prevost's frontier, inch by inch, had so far been successful thanks to Brock's initiative and the catalytic presence of the Indian warriors. But if Prevost sought somehow to play down the conflict, he was irretrievably allied to men who saw it as a bloody and terminal contest, once joined. That was made evident when, on the day Hull surrendered, the small garrison of the remote American Fort Dearborn, where Chicago now stands, was pounced upon by Potawatomi warriors who had heard of the capture of Mackinac. The fight took place as the garrison was evacuating the fort, and it was a merciless affair in which the American survivors were led off into captivity. To the tribes Tecumseh courted for his federation, it had seemed – until the Dearborn–Prevost armistice – that making common cause with the redcoat was a policy that would bear fruit.

At this point the scene of the fighting had shifted to the western end of Lake Erie again, as President Madison had set aside the armistice, and the opportunity to rebuild their forces had given the Americans a renewed opportunity for success after the Detroit disaster. Stretching southwestward from the end of Lake Erie was a marshy, difficult area – the "Black Swamp." In this area was the battle site of Fallen Timbers, and the winding course of

Fort Dearborn, on the site of Chicago, was the scene of an attack by western Indians early in the war, after news had spread about the capture of Mackinac and other British successes. The fort's withdrawing garrison was cut to pieces by the warriors when it responded to an order from William Hull to retire to Fort Wayne, Indiana.

the Maumee River. At the upper end of the Maumee River Valley stood the American post of Fort Wayne, which had been Muir's target, and as September began to turn the leaves to red and gold Tecumseh's warriors set out southwestward from Fort Malden to attack several posts which were outliers of Fort Wayne. One of these was Pigeon Roost, where a slaughter – of a brutal pattern that would become all too common – took place on September 3.

By September 6 the warriors were at Fort Wayne, but the fort was not about to tumble into their hands. Harrison's appointment to gather enough men and take Detroit back meant that the popular and capable Indiana governor was stepping into the role in which Hull had failed. Harrison knew his enemy, however, and knew that the best men for such a fight were those who were as forest-wise and ferocious as Tecumseh's warriors. To find them, he turned to the frontier state of Kentucky, where he held a militia commission of major general, and assembled a capable force of the kind of men he wanted, and then added militias from Virginia and Pennsylvania. He convinced Washington to name him supreme commander of the army of the Northwest, and set off to relieve Fort Wayne as a first step towards the retaking of Detroit, although the bumbling American secretary of war, Dr. Eustis, had separately commissioned James Winchester to lead federal troops to Fort Wayne. Harrison knew that his Kentuckians and the Indiana militia would follow him, but that they disliked Winchester; he cemented his right to command by winning the race with Winchester to Fort Wayne on September 12 in a decisive manner that Isaac Brock – in many ways a similar man – would have admired. The hovering warriors faded away at the arrival of Harrison's huge force and, when Winchester arrived on the scene, Harrison sent him on with his two thousand regular soldiers farther down the Maumee River. There, at a set of rapids, they were to wait out the fall and winter and be ready for a decisive campaign Harrison was planning for the Detroit frontier in 1813.

Meanwhile at Fort Malden, the need was growing for the British to take action to relieve the concerns of their Indian allies, and Henry Procter was determined to regain the offensive. As Harrison and Winchester moved towards Fort Wayne, Adam Muir was sent off again, with a thousand redcoats and warriors and orders, to establish a firm position on the Maumee River. Procter himself had put a British post at the small settlement of Frenchtown, on the Raisin River, which ran into Lake Erie just above the Maumee, and had explored ahead as far as the rapids towards which Winchester was advancing. Muir had penetrated well above the rapids, then pulled back to a ruined log stockade, Fort Defiance, when, on September 25, his scouts ran into the patrols ahead of Winchester's force. Winchester halted, and fortified his camp rather than attacking Muir's position, and, after a tense standoff in which each force

William Henry Harrison, governor of Indiana Territory, shown in the uniform of an American general in this portrait by Charles Willson Peale. Resolute and ruthless in his pursuit of American expansion and the destruction of Indian power, he was Tecumseh's most implacable foe, while acknowledging the extraordinary qualities of the Shawnee chief. His victory over Tecumseh eventually took him to the White House, but he died shortly after taking office.

Henry Procter, British commander at Fort Malden, had the unenviable task of holding the Detroit frontier with little support from Prevost. He suffered from an inability to live up to the standard Brock had set and the expectations of the warriors. His evacuation of Fort Malden and his defeat at Moraviantown, where Tecumseh died, would bring an end to his career.

expected the other to materialize out of the treeline, Muir retired to Fort Malden. Harrison and Winchester settled in on the Maumee and planned the coming campaign. As the snows began to fall on the western theatre of the war, an American lance was pointed at the Canadian frontier on the Detroit River, awaiting the spring to be thrown home. Tecumseh was left to wonder at his red-coated allies, who could demonstrate such dogged bravery, yet be subservient to distant men – men unaware of what opportunities could be lost. Perhaps, fatally, they already had been.

With Harrison injecting new energy and promise into the western campaign, Washington could also take comfort in the continuing success of its seamen. On September 26, the day after Muir's scouts ran into Winchester's men, Commodore Isaac Chauncey, USN, said farewell to his family and set off on the Hudson River steamboat for Albany, where he was to meet with Henry Dearborn. Following that meeting, he was to take in hand American naval fortunes on the Great Lakes. The news of the double disasters of Mackinac and Detroit had led President Madison and his cabinet to give two key orders: one was to set in motion the forces of Harrison

Isaac Chauncey was a capable and experienced American naval officer and, within months of assuming command at Sackets Harbor, he had control of Lake Ontario.

The brig Oneida, *pictured here off Sackets Harbor, was Chauncey's most effective vessel in the early part of the war. As the war progressed, a building race led to both sides launching or planning huge, 100-gun warships that would dwarf the corvette-sized* Oneida.

and Winchester towards Detroit; the second was to determine that United States naval squadrons be created on Lakes Ontario and Erie, to seize and maintain control of them. The small but enormously competent frigate force of the USN, which was repeatedly humiliating the Royal Navy, provided employment for only a relative few of the skilled officers and men the navy commanded, and the British blockade of the coast – and American shipping – meant that additional prime seamen, all of whom would bring a greater level of training to the job than the hapless crews of the Provincial Marine, would be available to man the squadrons. Chauncey was a Connecticut native with a solid career record, although little actual experience of action, and he brought to the task enthusiasm and a needed talent for administration. That those qualities would be sorely tested was evident from the beginning, as the Provincial Marine vessels were superior to those of the United States Navy in numbers and guns – on paper at least. Woolsey and his hundred men at Sackets Harbor had the *Oneida* and a lake schooner or two, while on Lake Erie there was virtually nothing to contest the *Queen Charlotte*. Only the relative ineffectiveness of the Provincial Marine prevented total British domination of the lakes.

Chauncey's actions were swift in coming. One hundred and fifty ship-wrights, supervised by the talented Scot immigrant Henry Eckford, were sent off to build a squadron at Sackets Harbor, and to convert merchant schooners that Woolsey had bought into warships. Seamen and marine volunteers were sent from blockaded frigates on the eastern seaboard, accompanied by capable young officers eager for action. One of them, Lieutenant Jesse Elliott, demonstrated this energy by travelling to Lake Erie and, on October 8, 1812, taking the armed British vessels *Caledonia* and *Detroit* – Hull's former *Adams* – in a "cutting out" expedition under the guns of the British post at Fort Erie, which stood where Lake Erie empties into the Niagara River. A naval yard was set up on that lake, at Black Rock, New York, a short distance from Buffalo, and a river of naval supplies began to move north.

As the fall of 1812 deepened, Chauncey determined to focus his efforts on Lake Ontario, where the Provincial Marine squadron at Kingston formed the greatest obstacle to American dominance of the lake, and to capture the British posts at either end of it. It would not be until early November that Chauncey would meet his enemy for the first time, in incidents that demonstrated once more that the Provincial Marine was not going to be the match of the United States Navy. Returning to Sackets Harbor after several successful encounters, Chauncey could rightly feel that, as the snows began to fall, he was in virtual command of Lake Ontario.

The new energy on the western frontier and on the lakes had not been matched by Henry Dearborn's efforts to probe on his Niagara and Champlain fronts of action. The American plan still called for diversionary effort on the Niagara frontier to mask a thrust up the Champlain–Richelieu Valley. Dearborn dutifully gave orders to move his troops to a staging point at Plattsburg, on the west shore of Lake Champlain, while writing to his inexperienced militia general in command on the Niagara frontier to "embrace the first practicable opportunity for effecting a forward movement." Major General Stephen Van Rensselaer had under his command a heterogeneous

Stephen Van Rensselaer, a militia officer placed in command of American forces on the Niagara, was bedevilled by the hostility of an American regular officer there, Alexander Smyth. Van Rensselaer's command would end with the failure of the Queenston Heights invasion attempt.

body of militia and a slowly growing force of regular federal troops under Brigadier General Alexander Smyth. Smyth and Van Rensselaer experienced the same relationship of a professional soldier with a militia officer that Harrison and Winchester suffered; but Van Rensselaer was no Harrison, and his preparations for some kind of "forward movement" across the Niagara River that fall were bedevilled by Smyth's passive resistance to any kind of meaningful cooperation. When Isaac Brock returned to the shores of Lake Ontario from Detroit, he found the militia more ardent in their desire to serve. The Iroquois of the Grand River reservation had also decided to abandon neutrality and take up the old alliance with the redcoats again. However, Prevost's limitations had meant that Brock was not able to do what he had done at Detroit: launch a sudden and decisive attack on the building American forces on the far shore. As Brock re-established himself at York and at Fort George, in what was then Newark, Upper Canada (and is now Niagara-on-the-Lake), and as the fall deepened, he was concerned that Van Rensselaer was planning an assault before the snows came. While Brock had every confidence in his relatively few redcoat regulars, particularly his own hard-drinking 49th Regiment of Foot, he was still uncertain of the loyalties and abilities of his militiamen – even after Detroit – since so many were virtually as American as his enemy.

On October 10, Van Rensselaer received an inaccurate report that Brock and much of his Fort George garrison had left for the Detroit frontier, and the American decided that, if ever there was a time to risk the "forward movement," it was now. His first move was to send a small force in boats from Lewiston, New York, to the Canadian village at Queenston, barely two hundred yards away across the rushing river. The attempt, in the pre-dawn gloom of October 11, ended in blundering chaos and was called off.

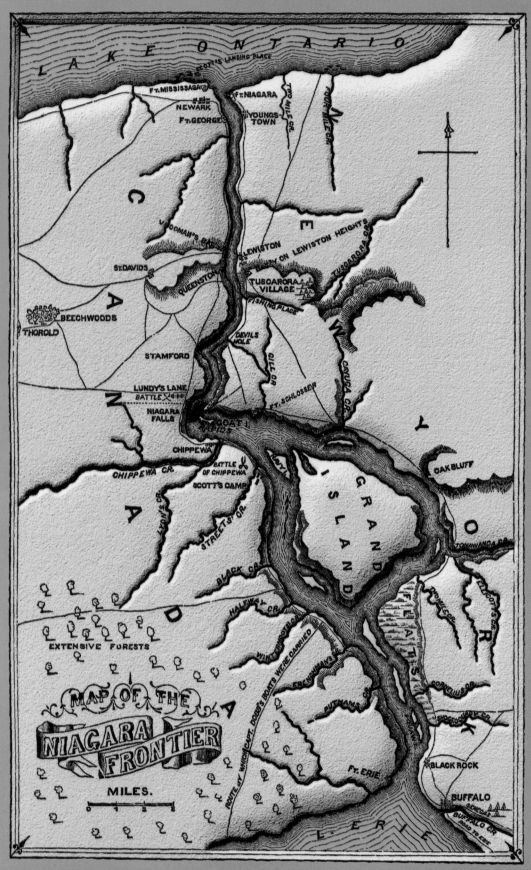

The fought-over Niagara frontier. By the end of the war its settlements and communities on both sides were blackened ruins from Lake Ontario to Lake Erie. It was the scene of the bloodiest and least-conclusive fighting of the war.

A second attempt was made two days later, and this time, in the early light of October 13, a party of just two hundred regular infantry and militia volunteers got across to Queenston under the command of Van Rensselaer's nephew, Joseph. The Queenston detachment of three hundred British infantry, under Captain James Dennis, were alerted to the landing and formed quickly enough to throw back the younger Van Rensselaer's first attempt to rush the heights above Queenston, where a small gun battery stood, protected by one hundred men under a Captain Williams. The Americans hung on grimly to their landing area after this first repulse, blazing away volley for volley with Dennis's men. Behind the beachhead, boat crews lathered to row more men over against the rushing current and, as the wet gloom of the October day lightened, the bang and thump of the musketry and of Williams's gun battery carried down the river gorge to Fort George, rousing Brock.

Brock was soon galloping south along the cart track towards Queenston and the distant sounds of battle, having left orders for General Roger Sheaffe, his second-in-command, to gather every man available and follow

The Harbour at Niagara, 1811. *The mouth of the Niagara River on Lake Ontario was a vital post, first held by the French in the seventeenth century. Ships anchoring close to either shore had to contend with the powerful current sweeping down the Niagara Gorge from the Falls.*

after him. It is an image engraved in the popular history of Canada: the blue cloak billowing back from the scarlet uniform coat and white breeches above tall boots, the dark clouds scudding overhead as the horse's hooves beat on against the wet earth. It did not take him long to arrive at the scene and to witness the efforts the Americans were putting into getting more troops ashore. Determining that the landing was a serious assault attempt, Brock ordered Williams to bring his company down off the heights and join the battle at the landing place, leaving a few men with the gun. It was a fateful decision.

Colonel Joseph Van Rensselaer was quick to seize the opportunity, and, with a Lewiston guide who knew his way about on the Canadian shore, he sent two companies of the United States 13th Infantry Regiment under Captain John Wool to find a path to the heights. They found it, and so quickly that they took the gun and almost caught Brock himself from behind in the process. The blue-coated American infantry burst out of the woods and seized the little gun battery, while, barely a shot away, Brock escaped on foot down the hill, leading his horse.

The British situation was now grave. Dennis's defenders in Queenston were being pushed back by the bluecoats swarming ashore, and Sheaffe

A View of Niagara.
This view from Queenston Heights looks north to Lake Ontario. The community of Queenston lies below the heights, to the left, and Lewiston, New York, is to the right. The American assault boats in 1812 left from the American shore almost directly below where the British infantrymen are sitting.

and the reinforcements were still miles away. Now, Wool's two companies held the heights where Williams's men had been, putting in peril the defenders clustering in the village below. Brock's response was instinctive, and characteristic. Wool was there, his infantry firing into Williams's and Dennis's men, and Brock chose to attack him head-on. Calling up Williams's company of the 49th Foot, he formed them in line and led them in a scrambling assault up the heights towards Wool's men, slithering on the wet grass and mud under the leaden sky.

But Wool's infantry were not untrained militia, and Wool was not Hull. The long flintlock muskets banged against the Americans' shoulders, and a torrent of fire poured down on the struggling 49th men, halting and breaking the charge. They fell back, their dead tumbling around them, until Brock rallied them and urged them back up the hill. They climbed again, the musket balls humming like bees around them, thumping here and there into a crumpling figure. Brock was ahead now, his sword drawn, calling to his men to use the bayonet. Then, just under a hundred yards from Wool's line, a ball found its mark squarely in Brock's chest. He fell on the muddy slope, whispering to the men who rushed to kneel by him that his death should be hidden, so as not to discourage the troops. He died within moments. The charge faltered, and then failed, and, with Wool's musketry blazing down at them, the men of the 49th fell back down the bloodied hill, Brock's body in their arms.

As they stumbled, muddy and blood-smeared and in tears, into Queenston village, Brock's aide, John MacDonnell, arrived and tried to maintain the defence. He had brought with him two companies of militia, and he thrust them, together with the remnants of Williams's men, in a rough line, ordered the bayonets fixed on the "Brown Bess" muskets, and led them back up the hill on which Brock had died, wide-eyed militiamen scrambling beside the grieving, angry men of the 49th. Now Wool's men held their fire until MacDonnell, the 49th, and the Canadian militiamen were barely fifty feet away; then a thunderous volley crashed out. Williams and MacDonnell fell, the latter mortally wounded, and, as the hill rang with the screams of wounded men writhing on the slope, the attack withered, leaving Wool in command of his prize. His climb to the heights and the death of Brock put a shattering victory within sight of Van Rensselaer's "forward movement."

Below, in Queenston, James Dennis fought to be heard over the din of

A well-known rendering of the battle of Queenston Heights by a participant, Major James Dennis. Dennis's work is a composite scene showing a number of events at once. The image, showing the American struggle to gain the Heights (left) and the ordered lines of advancing British and Canadians, still in their white summer trousers, suggests the drama of the contest.

the musket blasts and the shouted orders, the cries of the injured. He pulled his men back from where they had been resisting the main landing force, and grouped them with the dazed and muddy survivors of the two deadly charges up the hill. Sensibly, he led them in an orderly retreat a short distance downriver to Vrooman's Point, there to await Sheaffe's arrival, rather than let them be needlessly overwhelmed by the mass of blue now filling Queenston.

Before long, Wool had been joined atop the heights by almost a thousand men, and a Brigadier General Wadsworth, who now took command. But, even as they secured their position, they had to repel an attack by a whooping party of Indian warriors, who had arrived ahead of Sheaffe. That attack was heard by almost two thousand American militia members who were waiting on the far shore to cross, and, abruptly, not a man would move to the boats. The professional American soldiers on the Canadian shore were suddenly on their own.

A popular depiction of Brock's death, done many years later. The artist has erred in details of uniform, and has chosen to show Brock calling out for the York volunteers to press on. In reality, Brock only whispered that his death should be hidden so as not to upset the troops. However, the cloaking smoke of gunfire and the rushing assault of the infantry capture in part the feeling of the struggle.

AN AWFUL AND EVENTFUL CONTEST" — 83

Winfield Scott was one of the most effective of the American commanders. Audacious and courageous, he knew the value of training and preparation. His leadership would be a major factor in the capture of Fort George in 1813, and his creation of the grey-clad brigade that won at Chippewa in 1814 would restore a sense of honour to the regular United States Army. His love of precision and detail led to his nickname of "Old Fuss and Feathers," and he would remain the pre-eminent American soldier until the coming of the American Civil War.

Now Roger Sheaffe arrived with more British regulars and militia, followed by artillery and cavalry. It was clear that a frontal assault up a wet and muddied slope against a height of land occupied by a thousand well-trained and highly motivated defenders was suicidal. Instead, Sheaffe swung his column west, to where he could approach the heights on more level ground, screened by trees. The approach was not seen by the Americans on the heights until a sudden skirmish of fire erupted on the Americans' left flank, followed by the startling appearance of a British and Canadian battle line, bayonets gleaming in the dull October light, coming like a red wave out of the dark treeline a short distance away and moving steadily in, while the air was rent with the warriors' cries. Their ammunition spent, the Americans put up a brief resistance until they were crowded back against the river's edge of the heights, and a young American officer, Winfield Scott, who would go on to a remarkable destiny, waved a white neckcloth on a sword point in surrender. Panic had seized some of the Americans at the apparent approach of massacre, and many died tumbling down the precipice to the river, from whence the American boatmen had fled back to the American shore.

Sheaffe's force was no larger than the American one, but prudent tactics, the Americans' exhausted ammunition supply, and the incalculable effect of the warriors' presence had handed Sheaffe and his men a victory. Queenston Heights would now join Mackinac and Detroit in the litany of failures that was the American military effort to secure Canada in 1812. There were no references now to mere matters of marching.

But the architect of the aggressive defence that had made possible this result died in this final major encounter of 1812, a victim, some would say, of injudicious audacity that deprived his country – both Britain and the Canadas – of one of its defensive pillars of spirit and of leadership. Tecumseh, too, lost much in Brock's death, for he lost the most powerful and honourable advocate of the Indian homeland that was the rightful price of the warriors' defence of Canada. No one would speak with such a voice again.

Brock died in heroism, both facing his enemy and leading men who adored him. He would never know that, three days before his death, he had been knighted by the king for his taking of Detroit. A monument would later be built on the site of his death by the country he had fought so well to defend. But the loss was too great, almost irreparable, and Canada suffered for it in the following two years of war. It was left to Anne Prevost to give the simplest and most wistful of eulogies for this brave man, who had died, perhaps unwisely, in the heroic mould he so admired.

Brock's monument atop Queenston Heights, seen here in 1860, was a replacement for one that had been erected there in 1824, containing Brock's and MacDonnell's bodies. The first monument was destroyed, possibly by Fenians.

An Express brought the news of the Battle of Queenstown, and the death of our noble defender, General Brock. I had never seen him, but all felt as if they had lost a friend. Had he lived how different everything might have turned out. His energy and talents were invaluable to my Father, for it was impossible for one individual to watch over both Upper and Lower Canada in the way that was necessary for their complete defence. This excellent officer was only "too prodigal of life" – he fell while leading on the Grenadiers of the 49th Regiment: his own favourite corps. If he had but reserved his personal exertions till the reinforcements came up – which ultimately drove back the invaders – his Country might have had him still. A General ought sometimes to recollect how valuable his life is to his army.

– Journal of Anne Prevost, later addition to entry for October 22, 1812

CHAPTER TWO

"To leave our bones upon them"

AMERICAN SUCCESS IN UPPER CANADA

THE DEATH OF ISAAC BROCK on the muddy slopes of Queenston brought a moment of universal mourning in the war. As he was interred in the ramparts of Fort George, guns banged out in echoing tribute from not only the British positions, but from Fort Niagara across the river. The slow succession of thunderlike blasts echoed up the Niagara Gorge, a solemn salute to a man and soldier loved by his troops and respected by his enemy. But with the honours and salutes done, the Americans turned their efforts again to assaulting the frontier for which Brock had fought.

Determined to regain the initiative, Henry Dearborn accepted Stephen Van Rensselaer's resignation, and turned now to Alexander Smyth, ordering him to carry out essentially the same sort of "forward movement" that had eluded Van Rensselaer. Smyth had chafed at working with the militia officer, and he decided that Dearborn was an irritant, and went over his head by writing to the distant secretary of war, William Eustis, while preparing a new attack across the Niagara River. Eustis was pleased to hear of the latter, but unreceptive to Smyth's assumptions of independence, telling Smyth to obey Dearborn's orders and get on with things. Dearborn urged Smyth to try again for a successful beachhead on the Canadian shore, directing him to ask the advice of his officers, and assuring him that there would be diversionary attacks along the St. Lawrence, which would keep British attention elsewhere.

As October closed and the brightly clad trees became gaunt skeletons against the leaden skies of November, Smyth prepared his plan. The disaster at Queenston had led to the departure of the New York militia – almost to a man – and the mixed bag of regular troops and other state militiamen who constituted Smyth's remaining force were sickly, ill clothed, badly housed, and in a near-mutinous state. The arrival of war promoter Peter Porter, in a brigadier general's uniform, to shore up enthusiasm merely produced a mob riot in Buffalo between pro- and anti-war factions. There was an air of tragicomic

Peter B. Porter of New York was a vocal War Hawk who received a generalship during the war and railed against ineffectual leadership, including that of Alexander Smyth, with whom he fought a sham duel. The failure of the war against Canada would be a bitter blow to him.

opera settling over the American forces on the Niagara, and Smyth added to it by issuing grandiloquent declarations that portrayed his miserable, suffering troops as heroic, well prepared, and superior in numbers and physical strength to the enemy. The grey days shortened, and, in the gloom and chill, Smyth's time was running out if he was to have any success before winter.

After Queenston, Roger Sheaffe and Stephen Van Rensselaer had agreed on a truce, which could be ended by the giving of thirty hours' notice by either side. As Smyth watched his New York militia stream away and planned an assault with his remaining men, Sheaffe and his officers tried to disperse their forces along the Niagara frontier in the best possible way to prevent an American surprise attack, all the while dealing with the homesickness of the Canadian militia and the tendency of the regular soldiery to vanish into an oblivion of rum at every opportunity. Sheaffe knew that Fort Erie, at the south end of the Niagara frontier, and Fort George at the north, would be the principal targets. Therefore, he spread his mixed regular and militia force along the river frontier and extended small posts west along the Lake Erie shore, and similarly along the Lake Ontario shore towards the heights of Burlington and the western corner of Lake Ontario. The main British force in Fort George, and a smaller garrison in Fort Erie, would hold these places, anchoring either end of the frontier. The grey, rain-soaked days darkened, and the waiting British and Canadians huddled in their barracks or round their campfires, watching the river.

Finally, on November 19, Smyth's messenger arrived on the Canadian shore with the news that the Americans were ending the armistice, a moment that revealed again the poignant mixture of gallantry and savagery that marked the war. Sheaffe and his officers assumed – correctly, it would turn out – that Smyth would try an assault farther south along the river, where the shore was lower and less of an obstacle than below the great falls. In an effort to distract him, Sheaffe had the guns of Fort George open a bombardment on Fort Niagara two days after the end of the armistice. Soon, the Americans were banging back. But Smyth waited several more days before finally making his move.

Then, just over four thousand regular infantry and militia marched in two columns to the little community of Black Rock, New York, across the river from Fort Erie. A few hours after midnight, on the bitterly chill night

of November 28, sodden with the wind-driven sleet and snow, the two columns of men crammed themselves into open boats and rowed for the Canadian side. One column was under the command of Lieutenant Colonel Charles Boerstler, and its task was to seize the bridge over the cart track running along the river's edge at Frenchman's Creek, just north of Fort Erie. This would prevent any immediate British advance against the landings from their positions at Chippewa, or farther north. The second column, under Colonel William Winder, was to capture British gun batteries set up across from Black Rock, and thereby allow Smyth to cross the dark, rushing river with the main body of his army. It was a relatively sound plan, had all worked as Smyth intended.

Thrashing across in the squally darkness, the threadbare infantry of Winder's force, with surprise on their side, fell on the British batteries and, in a short, confused struggle, overwhelmed two militia companies and a small body of regulars of Brock's 49th Foot. The British and Canadian survivors broke away into the night, leaving their artillery pieces, which

The shore road on the Canadian side of the Niagara frontier where the river opens out into Lake Erie was, as all roads were, a dusty cart track. Here, sportsmen fire at clouds of passenger pigeons, once innumerable but now extinct because of such hunting.

were now "spiked" – an iron rod or spike was driven into the vent to make each gun inoperable – and out of action. But here Winder's judgement failed him, and he allowed part of his force to row back to Black Rock with prisoners, while the remainder trudged off towards Fort Erie rather than remaining in the position they had been told to hold.

This party was pounced on by a British column that had been sent off from Fort Erie to see what was going on, and, after a few sputtering exchanges of volleys, the Americans quickly surrendered. Boerstler's men, rowing out of the darkness towards the shore at Frenchman's Creek, were spotted by alert sentries and greeted with a point-blank blast of artillery that shattered two boats, spilling the heavy-laden infantrymen into the lethally cold dark water. Boerstler turned back, towering geysers of water leaping up around his boats as his men rowed desperately for Black Rock. Smyth's preliminary move had failed. As daylight came, the British and Canadians returned to the captured gun battery, put the guns back into action, and peered through the snow and drizzle to watch for the next American move.

It came in the form of an extraordinary letter from Smyth to the senior British officer on the spot, Lieutenant Colonel Cecil Bisshop, demanding that Bisshop surrender Fort Erie. Smyth made a great display of embarking his main force in boats while Bisshop was considering this letter, but Bisshop was unmoved by Smyth's flights of prose, and the defenders sheltered their flintlocks from the miserable drizzle and waited silently. His bluff called, Smyth disembarked his exasperated troops and sent them back to their dank huts and tents. As if anxious to look the part but reluctant to play it, Smyth attempted a last embarkation of assault troops on the night of November 30, but the troops were tardy getting into the boats and, when daylight arrived to end any chance of surprise, Smyth called off the attack, and with it any invasion plans for the season. Humiliated, despised by his dispirited troops, Smyth was insulted publicly by the apoplectic Porter, dodged a furious mob outside his lodgings in Buffalo, and endured a sham duel with Porter before vanishing into obscurity. The war on the Niagara frontier was over for 1812.

In Albany, Dearborn meant to try to implement what was left of his grand plan. His force at Albany was larger than either Hull's or Van Rensselaer's had been, but it had been inactive as these two men marched into disaster. Now, with Smyth's attack from Black Rock distracting the British, Dearborn had a last possibility of action against Montreal, and – a reluctant, grossly overweight, and uncertain figure – he set off with his army to Plattsburg, and on northward, the troops trudging up the muddy cart track to the border in the same November gloom and rain that had cloaked Smyth. In the lead was the regiment of Colonel Zebulon Pike, and behind the regular infantry followed a body of militia reluctant to cross into Canada – a sentiment that was becoming consistent. By November 19 the American force was at Champlain, New York. Soon thereafter, an advance party crossed into Canadian territory and reached the banks of the Lacolle River. Across the narrow stream waited a small force of defenders commanded by a vigorous, Canadian-born officer, Charles-Michel d'Irumberry de Salaberry, and made up of detachments of the grey-clad regulars of the Canadian Voltigeurs, Indian warriors, and local militia. They had not long to wait, as the American advance party splashed across the river in the pre-dawn dark of November 20. The Canadians were alert, and a blaze of musketry greeted the advance.

In the roiling gunsmoke and a heavy morning mist the Americans became disoriented. With the warriors' whoops echoing around them, they broke into groups and began firing on one another, until bugles sounded the retreat. The powerful American force could have overwhelmed the little band of Canadians in minutes; instead, the surprised Voltigeurs and their companions watched the Americans stumble off into the mist and back across the river, where they re-formed their columns and marched off south, leaving the dark shores of the Lacolle to the Canadians. It was the capstone of failure to a disastrous American prosecution of the land war against Canada, and they had discovered that the enemy to the north were tenacious, capable, and intent on defending every inch.

If the campaign to conquer the Canadas was becoming a disastrous humiliation to the army, the United States Navy provided a contrasting beacon of success. It had no chance of challenging the overall might of the Royal Navy, but in single-ship actions the story was very different. On October 25, the American frigate *United States*, 44 guns, defeated HMS *Macedonian*,

Zebulon Pike's name was given to a western mountain in recognition of his early surveying work. His regiment would later be present at the taking of York, and he would be killed there, while questioning a British prisoner, by a stone falling from an exploding powder magazine.

The "Provincial Corps of Light Infantry," or Canadian Voltigeurs, were raised and trained to regular army standards by Charles de Salaberry. The corps was almost entirely recruited in French Canada and would fight effectively during the war, notably at Chateauguay and Crysler's Farm.

38 guns, in what was rapidly becoming routine American success. A week earlier, the *Wasp*, 18 guns, had taken *Frolic*, 18 guns – only to be lost herself to HMS *Poictiers* – and the month of December would bring the victory of *Constitution*, 44 guns, over HMS *Java*, 38 guns.

Meanwhile, on Lake Ontario, Isaac Chauncey had succeeded in readying his squadron for its first series of challenges of the Provincial Marine's control of the lake. On November 8, 1812, led by the brig *Oneida*, Chauncey's little fleet of schooner-sized vessels sailed from Sackets Harbor, New York. The next morning, after riding at anchor in the lee of Main Duck Island, at the eastern end of the lake, Chauncey discovered Hugh Earl's flagship, *Royal George*, inbound to Kingston from the west. Chauncey set off in hot pursuit, but in light winds *Royal George* kept ahead of *Oneida* and the schooners. Earl took the corvette into the gap between Prince Edward Peninsula and Amherst Island, and escaped Chauncey as night fell by sailing east along the North Channel towards Kingston. But Chauncey persisted. The squadron anchored for the night, and next morning closed on Kingston along the shoreline, with *Royal George* visible at anchor in the Kingston Channel ahead. Until wind and uncertainty about shoals led Chauncey to call off the attack, his squadron engaged in a hot gunnery duel with the Kingston shore

With her defeat of HMS Java, USS Constitution *added to her list of battle honours. Constitution's ability to resist the impact of enemy fire led to her being nicknamed "Old Ironsides" by her crew.*

Isaac Chauncey's initial efforts to dominate the waters of Lake Ontario led to the virtual driving of British vessels off the lake by his roving warships. Here, in a contemporary sketch, American schooners pursue their British quarry in the vicinity of Amherst Island.

batteries and the *Royal George,* which was forced to work up into Kingston harbour to escape Chauncey's fire.

Leaving Kingston, Chauncey pursued another Provincial Marine vessel, the *Governor Simcoe,* which escaped only by running in close to shore, damaging itself on a shoal in the process. Returning to his Main Duck Island anchorage, Chauncey was forced to leave there on November 12 when a gale blew up. But in four days, he had run the flagship of the British lake fleet right into its home port, bombarded the shore, and made it evident that, for the moment, the lake was his to roam at will. He returned to Sackets Harbor, aware that eleven weeks after receiving his orders he had established American control of Lake Ontario.

The end of navigation season was crowned by the launch of the corvette *Madison* – which was more than a match for *Royal George* – at Sackets Harbor. In the face of this, Sir George Prevost sent off to Kingston a trained eye in the form of Captain Andrew Gray to assess the ability of the Provincial Marine to meet the threat, and as the year closed he was recommending everything from an attack over the ice on Sackets Harbor to a fortification and shipbuilding program at Kingston and York. The stakes were to be raised in the crucial naval contest for control of the lakes.

On the Atlantic coast, the depredations of American privateers were being matched by Nova Scotia and New Brunswick vessels, which made fortunes for their owners as they captured American merchant vessels. However, side by side with this cousinly little war, American merchants were carrying out a clandestine trade with Nova Scotia which suggested that, however real their argument might have been with the high-handed Royal Navy and its policy of ship arrests and impressment, trading with Canada was far more attractive and natural than the blood and conquest of "Mr. Madison's War." Their feelings were most clearly stated in the words of federalist Josiah Quincy, who in Congress described the war against Canada as a

cruel, wanton, senseless and wicked attack, in which neither plunder nor glory was to be attained upon an unoffending people bound to us by ties of blood and good neighbourhood, undertaken for the punishment over their shoulders of another people three thousand miles away by young politicians fluttering and cackling on the floor of the House, [to whom] reason, justice, pity were nothing, revenge everything.

But the feelings of men like Quincy were not in ascendancy in Washington, where the War Hawks held sway, and these latter were determined to profit from the lessons of 1812 and use the considerable resources of the United States, in men and goods, to win the war. The toughness and competence of the three enemy partners – the warrior, the redcoat, and the best of the Canadian militiaman – had been a rude shock. But the War Hawks were determined to make 1813 the year of success.

Josiah Quincy was a federalist and a vocal opponent of the Canadian war.

For the British, the heady atmosphere of triumph in midsummer had waned, even as their successes continued. Brock's death at Queenston had taken from the Canadian defence the voice that equalled Tecumseh's, and the warrior stood alone, unsure of the lesser men who had replaced

Brock. In the Old Northwest, the Long Knives were building for another assault under Harrison and Winchester in the New Year, and in better times Tecumseh would have been at the long American supply trains like a circling mountain lion. But illness befell him, and he retired to an encampment by the Wabash River in Indiana, near what remained of Prophet's Town. There he chafed at his enforced inactivity, sending messages to the various tribes in and about the theatre of war, urging them to join the British. To the British, with Brock gone, Tecumseh sent messages warning them not to sign a separate peace with the Americans, and so abandon the Indians, for he had had a premonition that this might happen now that Brock's voice could no longer speak for Indian rights. Over the winter of 1812–1813, he recovered slowly from his sickness, the Americans leaving his encampment strangely unmolested, warriors rallying to him daily. Then, in mid-January, Tecumseh received electrifying news of another major disaster to American arms.

On the Maumee River, Winchester's advance force of slightly more than one thousand men had shivered through the winter, waiting for the spring campaign. In early January, Winchester determined to move, and, although Harrison had wanted the entire army to advance together over the Detroit River ice to take Fort Malden, Winchester went on ahead with an advance party of several hundred men to Frenchtown, on the Raisin River. He had driven out of it a small party of British regulars and Indians, who brought word of Winchester's advance on January 19 to Colonel Henry Procter at Fort Malden. To Procter's credit, he realized that a new enemy presence a mere thirty miles south of Fort Malden would have to be countered, and so he crossed to Brownstown, just north of Frenchtown, and assembled a striking force. He had brought every available man from Fort Malden, and that gave him just under six hundred British infantry, seven hundred Indian warriors under the chief Roundhead, and a supporting battery of six field guns. Movement was difficult in the deep snow and the cold, but Procter and Roundhead set out immediately for Frenchtown, where they arrived at the break of dawn. The Americans were completely unaware of Procter's arrival: no sentries had been posted to watch the snow-covered road to the north.

The British formed a line and advanced through the deep snow towards the cluster of huts and tents, mounted warriors and Canadian militia pressing forward on the flanks. The American infantry stumbled out of their quarters, but formed quickly, delivering well-aimed volleys into the advancing tight line of greatcoat-clad figures. The British began to fall, gaps opening in the formation as they came on. But on the flanks, the whooping warriors and Canadians pressed in, and the American right flank broke and tried to run under the fierce rush of Roundhead's mounted men, who cut them down with tomahawks as they ran. Winchester arrived, dishevelled and half dressed, only to be immediately captured and brought to Procter, who convinced him to call on his surviving men to surrender.

They did so, but on the next day, when Procter pulled back to Fort Malden, fifty wounded Americans for whom he was responsible were left behind in houses at Frenchtown, where a party of intoxicated warriors massacred them in a horrifying rejection of Tecumseh's teachings on honourable warriorship. The American defeat was total – almost three hundred killed and six hundred captured – and it put an end to Harrison's plans to attack Malden over the ice. But the horror of the massacre gave the men of Harrison's waiting army a rallying cry that they would carry north: "Remember the Raisin!" It added a fiercer and more brutal edge to the American war against the warriors, if such was possible. But to Tecumseh, it sig-nalled that the British were still capable of defeating the Americans, even with Brock gone. More Indian allies made their way to Malden, and, with the spring, Tecumseh joined them.

Still smarting from the slaughter on the Raisin, the Americans began to prepare for 1813's conquest attempt with abler men – and

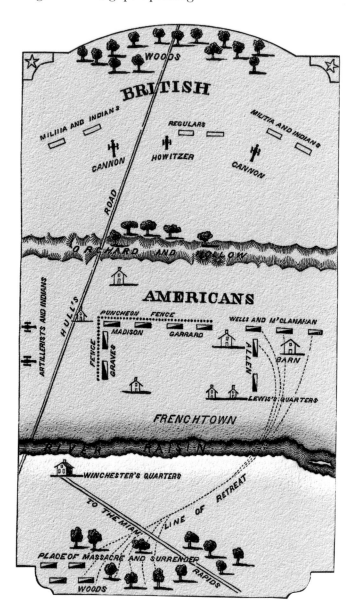

The deployments at Frenchtown, where Winchester's unpreparedness led to a defeat and the slaughter of American wounded and prisoners.

A crude but effective depiction of the massacre of the Americans following the Battle of Frenchtown. Procter's failure to ensure the safety of the Americans led to the killings, which hardened American resolve to destroy the warriors and their leadership, particularly Tecumseh. Ironically, Tecumseh always strove to prevent such wanton acts.

a growing arsenal. A man of War Hawk sympathy, John Armstrong, took over from Dr. Eustis as secretary of war, and, if he retained the same three-front strategy in his planning for 1813, he brought more energy and a wiser use of resources to the task. For Sir George Prevost, fretting in his Quebec citadel over his meagre resources, the coming season threatened to be a very worrisome one indeed. Britain was still engaged with Napoleon, and even if the United States could hurl greater resources into the war, the British could – or would – not.

Andrew Gray's grim report on the state of the decrepit Provincial Marine gave Prevost an idea as to what to do about holding Lake Ontario: ships could be built, if few, and some sailors found to man them. It was on land that he faced the greatest challenge. Along a thousand-mile border with a nation that, if pressed, could field a militia of more than a hundred thousand armed men familiar with weapons – if not with military ways – Prevost had six infantry regiments of several hundred men each, and an equal

number of Canadian regiments such as the Voltigeurs; a mass of untrained, sedentary militia mostly in Lower Canada; and the warriors. Commanding these forces was Roger Sheaffe, competent enough, but lacking Brock's charisma and inspired leadership. There were capable officers below him, like de Salaberry of the Voltigeurs, and Joseph Morrison of the Kingston garrison. But in the most vulnerable post, Fort Malden, Henry Procter had yet to prove he had the depth of judgement and the staying power Tecumseh and the Indian allies would require to keep their allegiance. Spring of 1813 was one of threatening portent for the Canadas, however successful 1812 had been. Prevost's alarm at Gray's report and Chauncey's control of Lake Ontario led him to beg the Royal Navy to take over the troubled Provincial Marine.

By the end of May an RN officer, Sir James Lucas Yeo, had arrived at Kingston with just under five hundred sailors and shipboard infantry, and was supervising the rush to build ships there, and at York, to match Chauncey. But Yeo would have to worry about Lake Erie as well. Whereas before there had been no United States naval presence on the lake, Chauncey had now sent a young USN officer, Oliver Perry, to build one. The growing American land threat, rebuffed once, was returning, supported by an active and capable navy on Lake Ontario and the threat of one on Lake Erie.

On the Detroit frontier, Harrison's competence and overwhelming force were beginning to turn the tide against Procter and Tecumseh. The savage defeat of Winchester on the Raisin had caused Harrison to halt his march towards the frozen surface of Lake Erie. Instead of proceeding with the attack on Fort Malden, he entrenched his main army on the Maumee River and called the encampment Fort Meigs. Procter knew

John Armstrong, American secretary of war from February 5, 1813, to August 30, 1814. Armstrong replaced William Eustis and brought a greater degree of energy and ability to the post of secretary of war. His downfall would come with the British burning of Washington and the public perception that he had done little to prepare for such a catastrophe.

Sir James Lucas Yeo, the competent and initially energetic Royal Navy officer who took command of the British naval forces at Kingston in 1813, including the army's Provincial Marine vessels. Yeo would grow increasingly cautious as the struggle progressed, and fearful of losing the war in a few hours by being defeated by Chauncey on Lake Ontario.

that Harrison's army would only grow larger before the summer campaign, and that he should strike him at Fort Meigs before that happened if he was to have any chance of forestalling the invasion. It was not until April, however, that winter ice eased on the lake enough for Procter to take away a small fleet of schooners and bateaux carrying almost a thousand regulars and militia, accompanied by an equal number of Tecumseh's warriors. With this impressive force went a small artillery battery.

On arrival at the mouth of the Maumee, the guns were off-loaded and began a march up the river, while the bateaux, crammed with soldiers, worked against the current. By May 1, Procter had established a position close to Fort Meigs, approached the fort, and began a bombardment.

This map shows the movements during the first attack on Fort Meigs, during which Dudley's portion of the American relief column was cut to pieces by the warriors.

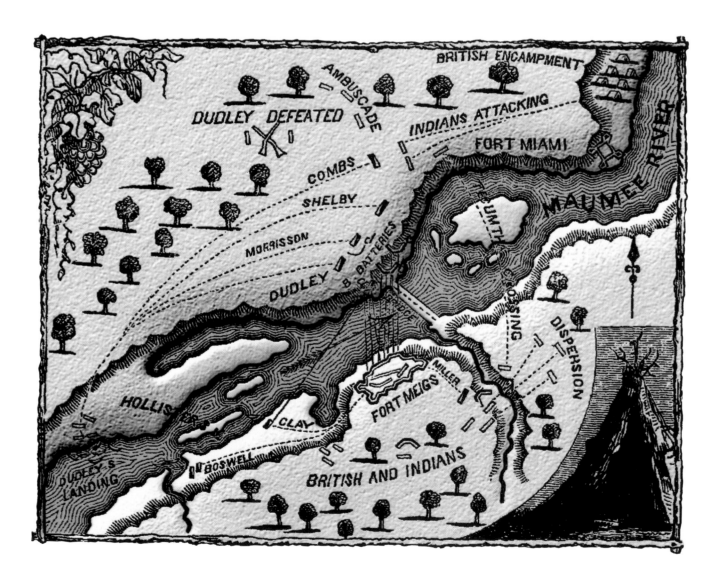

In similar circumstances at Detroit, William Hull had surrendered. But Harrison was cut from different cloth. He knew his walls could withstand the small British guns, and he also knew a relief column of some one thousand Kentucky militia under a Brigadier General Clay was only a short distance away upstream. Harrison dismissed Procter's call to surrender and sent a messenger off to find Clay, ordering him to attack the British from the rear, take the guns, and make for the fort. Harrison would then send out a force which, with Clay's, would destroy Procter.

On May 5, Clay's force arrived, split into columns that landed on both sides of the river above the fort, and clashed with the besiegers. One column overreached itself and was cut to pieces by the warriors, while the other had somewhat more success, capturing some of the British guns. Then, at a key moment, Harrison sent out his own sortie, and more guns were taken. If the siege appeared to have been broken, the fight was not, as the British and Indians came on again and inflicted heavy casualties on Harrison's men until the Americans got to shelter in the fort. Procter had a victory, of sorts, over Clay's column, but Harrison still held the fort, and Procter's force began to wither before his eyes. The Canadian militiamen by now were clamouring to leave, knowing they needed to seed their crops if there was to be any harvest. The warriors had plundered Clay's baggage train, and were uncontrollable, Tecumseh raging against them as they butchered American prisoners and revelled in the loot they had garnered. Faced with these insurmountable problems, Procter ended the attack and set off for Malden, while Harrison's men, bloody but unbowed, watched from the safety of their fort. The latter had won the day, and they knew it.

It was clear to Procter that Prevost would urge him to defend the distant Detroit frontier, all the while knowing that, if a serious second assault – such as the one Harrison was building towards – came, Prevost would abandon him rather than risk troops away from the heartland of Canada. Procter was left to do the best he could with his militia, his few redcoats – notably the 41st Foot – and Tecumseh's warriors. To his credit, he had realized that a forward defence, such as he used at Fort Meigs, was his only hope of postponing American attack – but could never prevent it. In time, the avalanche would overwhelm him, and when he returned from Fort Meigs he faced the grim reality of waiting for resources that would never come to Amherstburg in sufficient quantity. His army or the little naval force would have to beg

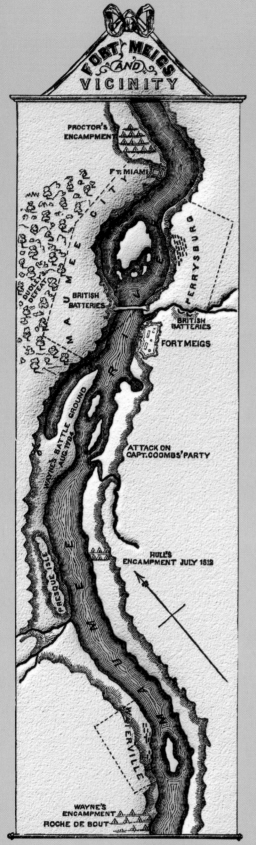

Fort Meigs's position on the bloodied banks of the
Maumee River was a short distance downriver
from the site of the 1794 Battle of Fallen Timbers.
Two efforts by the British to take it failed.

Fort Meigs's interior earthworks, shown in this reconstructive sketch done years later, prevented British artillery from inflicting any serious casualties on the garrison sheltering within.

for resources while Harrison prepared a hammer blow – and while Lake Erie threatened to become an American lake, with Perry's fleet taking shape behind the sandbar at Presque Isle, Pennsylvania. If Procter was morose and withdrawn during this time, he had reason to be.

Procter's woes on the Detroit frontier were those of a small fighter watching his opponent grow in size. On the Atlantic seaboard, the United States was beginning to feel the same sort of pressure from the huge Royal Navy. Admiral Sir George Cockburn's squadron had arrived off the coast, and had begun a series of raids and disturbances that the United States Navy was powerless to prevent. Ironically, the war was thus brought to those of the American population least supportive of it. However, the overwhelming strength of the Royal Navy meant that no American vessel was safe at sea,

Tecumseh's efforts to save American prisoners during the bloody aftermath of the failed first siege of Fort Meigs passed into American folklore as an example of his humanity.

since many capable seamen and officers were left idle. This allowed the Americans to send them off, relatively well supplied, to the Great Lakes. Here, the weight of preparation was turning in the Americans' favour as 1813 progressed.

Prevost's plea for help to the Royal Navy had given him a competent professional on Lake Ontario in the form of Sir James Yeo. But Prevost's principal worry, that the heartland of Canada – Quebec – would be taken by American thrusts down the St. Lawrence and up the Champlain Valley, led him to husband scarce resources close to home, and Yeo did the same at Kingston. If Procter had little support for his land forces, Robert Barclay, the Royal Navy officer sent to Amherstburg to build a little Lake Erie squadron, was left out on a similar limb. It was as if Prevost doled out to them the barest minimum of resources, hoping for success but expecting their loss. That any part of Canada west of Kingston was defended as well as it was against the blundering American power was owing largely to the spirit, resilience, and finally the desperation of the defenders. But that could only last so long.

Admiral Sir George Cockburn's British naval force roamed the Chesapeake at will and would land Ross's army for the capture and burning of Washington late in the war.

As the ice cleared from the lakes, and the patches of snow deep in the pine forests shrank from the heat of the sun, the American campaign against the middle of the three frontiers, the Niagara, renewed itself. In Albany, New York, Dearborn was considering the fact that Sheaffe had a few thousand men strung along the Niagara frontier between Fort George and Fort Erie, and a few hundred at York, the little Upper Canadian capital. Dearborn still clung to the principal strategy of using attacks on the Niagara and Detroit frontiers as a mask for the principal attack on Montreal and Quebec.

Chauncey had warned him that the U.S. command of Lake Ontario, vital for this strategy, would be at risk if Yeo at Kingston was allowed to improve the former Provincial Marine fleet that Chauncey temporarily dominated. Chauncey urged, and Secretary of War Armstrong agreed, that an attack across the ice in February of 1813 could take Kingston and end the naval threat. There had been practical use of over-ice attacks: Benjamin Forsyth's U.S. Rifle Regiment had attacked Elizabethtown (now Brockville) on the St. Lawrence this way on February 6, and, on February 22, a retaliatory raid had been launched against Ogdensburg, New York, from Fort Wellington at Prescott. Troops could march long distances in winter, as was being proven by the 104th Regiment of Foot, which had set off on February 16 from Fredericton, New Brunswick, on an epic snowshoe march that would take them all the way to Kingston in Upper Canada.

"Admiral Cockburn burning and plundering Havre de Grace," *done from a sketch taken on the spot. Thomas Jefferson's distrust of a standing military, and American belief in the effectiveness of a citizens' militia left the United States coastline defenceless against the capable and numerous British forces.*

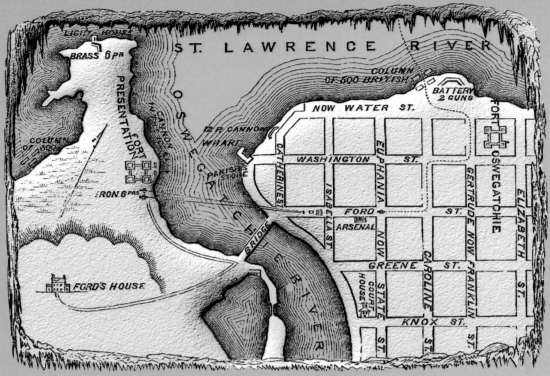

(Above) Across the river from the Canadian town of Prescott, Ogdensburg was attacked by British troops in February 1813. They marched across the frozen river in retaliation for an American raid on the neighbouring Canadian town of Elizabethtown (now Brockville). Citizens of Prescott and Ogdensburg did their best to minimize the war and maintain pre-war friendships and trade.

(Right) The American riflemen of Benjamin Forsyth's regiment, seen here behind conferring officers, carried out the Elizabethtown raid and precipitated the retaliatory raid on Ogdensburg.

However, Dearborn dithered until the ice was gone, and the Kingston attack was shelved. As Chauncey still pressed for action, Dearborn agreed to embark – at last – with troops to attack the poorly defended York, where new ships were known to be under construction for the Provincial Marine. Chauncey's squadron, packed with regular American infantry, some rifle-men, and a very seasick Dearborn, sailed in unopposed grandeur up the lake, arriving off York on April 27, 1813. The assault in overwhelming force brushed aside Sheaffe's few defenders, the largest number of casualties – including the death of Colonel Zebulon Pike – occurring when the British powder magazine exploded. Dearborn's men looted shops and homes, and put the little parliament buildings to the torch, an unnecessary series

This dramatic rendering of the 1837 winter march of the 43rd Regiment from New Brunswick to the Canadas captures the challenge of the remarkably similar trek made by the 104th Regiment some twenty-four years earlier.

of vandalisms that would cost the United States a humiliating price in the future.

Having done something inappropriate, Dearborn next threw away the opportunity produced by his capture of York. Rather than retain a force at York that cut off the Niagara frontier from British aid, he made off towards the Niagara shore with his loot, as if the attack had been nothing more than a raid. Behind him he left no garrison in the captured capital, but much ill will and an angry vengefulness.

Dearborn's next goal was to be the Niagara frontier, since in this effort he would benefit from Chauncey's control of the lake, but he became ill, and the plan for a landing to threaten Fort George and Newark (now

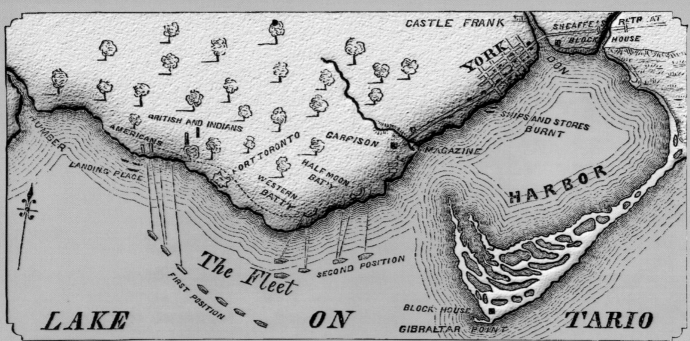

View of the assault landing west of the village of York. The British commander, Sheaffe, failed to repel the landing and fell back to the east towards Kingston, leaving York's citizens to negotiate with the invaders. Dearborn's troops began the pattern of looting and burning that would eventually lead to the torching of Washington.

An overview of the American fleet off York just before the successful assault. The ships are shown just to the east of their actual position.

The successful American assault landing that took York, the little Upper Canadian capital, suffered its greatest casualties when the British magazine exploded, showering troops with fragments of stone and debris.

Niagara-on-the-Lake) fell to Colonel Winfield Scott, a far abler officer than Dearborn. The success of Scott's plan demonstrated how command of the lake meant command of the land – if exploited properly.

Roger Sheaffe had retreated towards Kingston after being driven out of York, and the command of the Niagara frontier was in the hands of General John Vincent, who had slightly more than one thousand men in Fort George. On the morning of May 27, 1813, Scott selected a landing point on the Newark lakeshore where the guns of Fort George could not get a clear view. As his troops splashed ashore through a cloaking mist, Fort Niagara's guns made such an effort at bombardment that the wooden buildings in the fort, and some of the civilian homes, were soon afire. The landing was bitterly opposed, but Scott's brigades would not be denied as they poured ashore protected by a hail of covering shot from Chauncey's ships. Vincent's garrison lost almost five hundred men, and he withdrew

In this map (below), the close proximity of Fort George to Fort Niagara is evident. Winfield Scott's landing site, at the top of the map, was shielded from the guns of Fort George by the village of Newark, now Niagara-on-the-Lake.

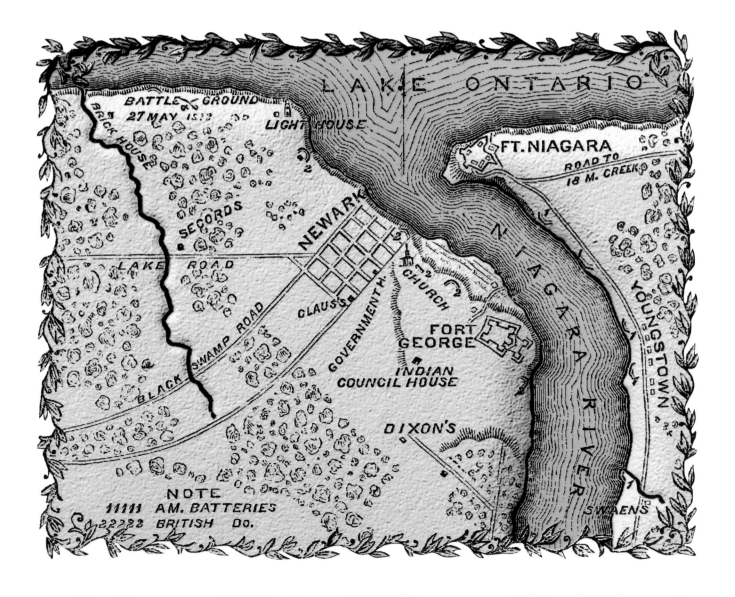

from the fort south and west to the little supply depot at Beaver Dams, sending orders for the detachments upriver at Queenston and Fort Erie to do the same. In a stroke, Dearborn's force had seized the principal British post on the Niagara frontier.

Vincent continued to retire northwestward, finally halting at Burlington at the western corner of Lake Ontario, where a commanding height of land could be fortified. Here he could still be supplied by cart track from Kingston through York, despite Chauncey's ships. Dearborn might have put Vincent in a hopeless situation, had he still held York. Nonetheless, American success seemed total. The capital had been taken, its defenders routed; the Niagara frontier's key post was abruptly in American hands; a squadron of five American ships trapped at Black Rock by Fort Erie's guns were now free to join Perry's growing squadron at Presque Isle, Pennsylvania; Harrison was building for his move on Procter; Chauncey controlled Lake Ontario; and Dearborn's main force in New York remained untouched and ready for the hammer blow at Prevost in Quebec. The

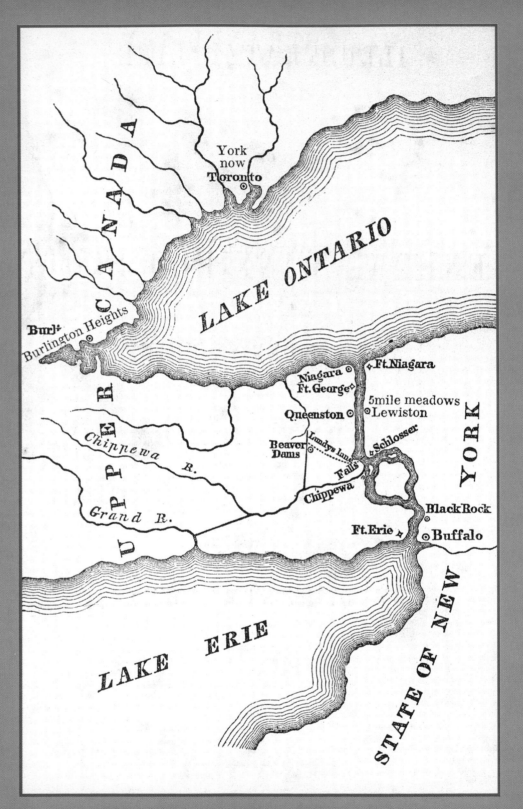

The Niagara frontier. With the capture of Fort George, the British retreated to Burlington Heights. Had Dearborn left a garrison in York, the British would have been cut off by land as well as water from help coming from Kingston or Lower Canada.

summer prospects for the United States were fair indeed. And if the Royal Navy blockade was humiliating and hurtful along the Atlantic coast, individual American ships had continued their pattern of success, as USS *Hornet*, 18 guns, defeated HMS *Peacock*, 18 guns, on February 24. British and Canadian fortunes would have to improve if disaster was to be avoided.

Dearborn sent off a force in pursuit of Vincent, and it edged its way carefully westward along the rutted roadway to Burlington beside Lake Ontario. Now was a moment of decision for Vincent. When would he have to give up all of Upper Canada as lost – including the hapless Procter and Tecumseh's warriors at Fort Malden – and set out for Kingston? The decision hinged on whether Dearborn would recover from his blunder and reoccupy York, and whether the Provincial Marine, which now was Yeo's command, and part of the Royal Navy, would appear to challenge Chauncey for control of the lake. As Dearborn's pursuing forces slowly approached Vincent's position at Burlington, Yeo was nowhere to be seen.

Yeo had arrived at Kingston only on May 5, and in his defence it is remarkable that by the end of the month he was in a position to sail with a force that would not simply generate mocking laughter in Chauncey's ships. The remarkable 104th Regiment of Foot had arrived in Kingston on May 12 after their epic trek, and Yeo had discussed with Prevost his first offensive move. Chauncey was known to be off with Dearborn at the western end of the lake. Yeo now considered whether to pursue him, or strike at his empty base at Sackets Harbor, where Hugh Earl had been driven away

USS Hornet *defeats* HMS Peacock *in another of the series of American single-ship victories that shocked the Royal Navy out of its complacency.*

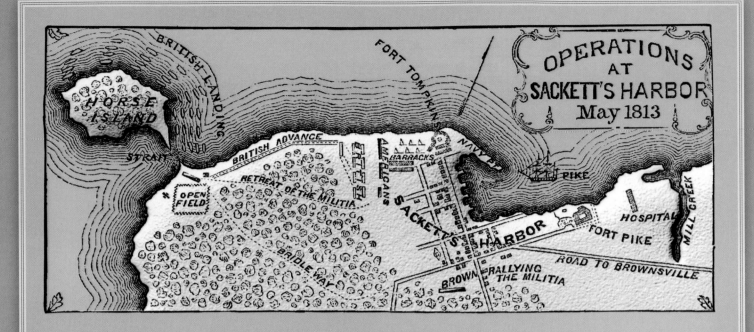

OPERATIONS AT SACKETT'S HARBOR May 1813

HORSE ISLAND
BRITISH LANDING
STRAIT
FORT TOMPKINS
NAVY
PIKE
BRITISH ADVANCE
RETREAT OF THE MILITIA
BRITISH
AMERICANS
BARRACKS
SACKETTS
OPEN FIELD
BRIDLE WAY
HARBOR
HOSPITAL
FORT PIKE
MILL CREEK
BROWN
RALLYING THE MILITIA
ROAD TO BROWNSVILLE

by Melancthon Woolsey the previous fall. Prevost came to Kingston full of caution and concern, but a decision was made nonetheless to attack Sackets Harbor with an assault landing of troops. Prevost would command the expedition in person, and Yeo, with energy and competence, got his newly formidable little squadron, packed with eager infantry, away from his anchorage on May 27 – the same day that Winfield Scott led his assault waves ashore at Newark.

Yeo's squadron beat out of Kingston and around Nine Mile Point, steering across the end of the lake to run into Sackets Harbor's bay by the next day. There, Yeo brought his ships to their anchor cables and called away the boats for the infantry. But Prevost now displayed a dismaying inability to know when caution had to be set aside in favour of initiative. The sight of a clutch of open rowing boats carrying American troops along the shore caused him to countermand Yeo's landing order and call the infantry back out of their boats. A party of Yeo's seamen and Indians went in anyway and captured more than half the boats, but Prevost still refused to stir, and the squadron rode at anchor without action off Sackets Harbor for the full day and succeeding night, giving the American defenders time to prepare with frantic haste for the assault. This long delay allowed the competent American commander, Jacob Brown, to muster more than a thousand infantry and militia to add to the startled few men who would have been overwhelmed by Yeo's attack had it gone in without Prevost's interference.

Finally, on the morning of May 29, having ensured his men would face a bloody and costly battle rather than a quick victory, Prevost allowed an attack to proceed against the now-alerted Americans, and at first it went well. The British and Canadian infantry splashed ashore at Horse Island, crossed a low causeway to the mainland, and broke an American line of infantry when the militiamen ran and left the regulars to be overwhelmed. Retiring, the Americans set fire to buildings and incomplete ships under construction, but they returned in time to put out these fires when, to their astonishment, Prevost called off the attack at the moment of success. The astounded – and eventually furious – British and Canadians were pulled back to their ships, and Yeo sailed away, leaving Brown to claim a victory Prevost had inexplicably handed him.

At the other end of the lake, the force Dearborn had sent off to Burlington after Vincent's retiring army halted to encamp near the present

(Opposite, top) A map showing operations during the abortive attack on Sackets Harbor in 1813. Initial British success was wasted by Sir George Prevost's refusal to press home the attack quickly and thoroughly, and by his order to retire when British troops were on the verge of victory.

(Opposite, bottom) Sunset at Sackets Harbor. Isaac Chauncey's efforts to develop a creditable lake squadron of the United States Navy at the small port of Sackets Harbor turned the village into an armed camp with a well-appointed dockyard.

town of Stoney Creek, only a few miles from Vincent's position. British scouts reported that the American camp was laid out awkwardly and without proper defensive preparations, and Lieutenant Colonel John Harvey, who took part in that scout, urged Vincent to attack the camp. Vincent agreed, and Harvey led seven hundred infantry of Brock's 49th Foot and the 8th (King's) Regiment in a confused and chaotic bayonet attack on the camp during the night of June 6. The British captured the American senior officers and a few guns, and made off back to Burlington, leaving the American force largely intact. Not intact, however, was its fighting fervour. The surviving officers ordered the American column into a retreat east towards Fort George, leaving their camp and the bodies of the dead. The retreat continued at a smart pace until the column reached Forty Mile Creek, about a third of the way back to Fort George, where it halted and recovered its nerve on meeting a reinforcement column sent out from Fort George.

But now naval power altered the picture, as it had for Dearborn at York and Fort George. Sir James Lucas Yeo – "the knight," as his enemy Chauncey called him – appeared offshore, having gone from Sackets Harbor to Kingston, taken aboard supplies and troops for Vincent, including the doughty 104th Foot, and sailed up the lake. Chauncey had returned to Sackets to marvel at Prevost's timidity, and now Yeo had the lake to himself. Two of his vessels were sent in to bombard the visible encampment at Forty Mile Creek on June 8. The Americans, fearing that Yeo was about to disgorge a horde of redcoats in a landing that would isolate them from Fort George, abandoned their camp – again – and marched briskly for Fort George, leaving a litter of arms, provisions, tentage, and gear all along the way.

Yeo's arrival had more impact than he might have imagined, for not only did the Lake Ontario column of Americans recoil into Fort George, but they gave hasty orders for the abandonment of the entire Niagara frontier, with the exception of the Fort George position. On June 9, Fort Erie was set on fire, and the American units on the frontier crowded into Fort George, beginning an industrious creation of extra earthworks round it, as if expecting a massive assault. It was an astonishing testimonial to not only the weakness of American leadership but to the power that control of the lake provided.

At Burlington, Vincent had gone from expecting to be overwhelmed by an American assault to seeing the American force retreat precipitously,

After the fall of Fort George, the pursuit of the retreating British by the Americans was halted and reversed when Vincent's British troops turned back and launched a night attack on the ill-prepared American encampment at Stoney Creek. C.W. Jefferys's drawing captures the feeling of the confused struggle, which sent the Americans back to Fort George, abandoning their tents and equipment.

harried by Yeo's ships. The ships also disembarked infantry reinforcements and needed supplies, including American supplies seized at the mouth of the Genesee River. On hearing that the Americans were to hold only Fort George on the Niagara frontier, Vincent determined to advance what he could of his small force, and he moved forward to Forty Mile Creek. From there, probing parties of scouts, infantry, and mounted troops went ahead and set up advance posts on the cart tracks leading to the Niagara River. One of these was at Beaver Dams, a short distance southwest of the hamlet

James FitzGibbon, who accepted the surrender of Boerstler's American column at Beaver Dams. The effective fighting of the Mohawk warriors brought victory to the British side.

of St. Davids, and was commanded by Lieutenant James FitzGibbon. There was much raiding and furtive skirmishing in the Niagara Peninsula, involving parties of American irregulars and Canadian renegades, but FitzGibbon's post at Beaver Dams threatened an encirclement of Fort George, and the American commander of the latter, John Boyd, determined that FitzGibbon had to be driven out.

A column of infantry with dragoon and artillery support was sent off under Lieutenant Colonel Charles Boerstler to march south to Queenston, then southwest for Beaver Dams and a surprise assault on FitzGibbon's position. In what has become a famous Canadian story, Boerstler's boastfulness

A WOMAN'S HEROISM:
THE LEGEND OF LAURA SECORD

The courageous trek of Queenston housewife Laura Secord through forest and marsh to warn James FitzGibbon at Beaver Dams of Boerstler's approach became justly enshrined in Canadian legend, even given the likelihood that the Mohawk warriors with FitzGibbon knew Boerstler was coming and were already preparing an ambush. In the first image, Secord is shown giving her warning to FitzGibbon much as it might have taken place, although some elements of costume are inaccurate. In the far more romantic second image, Secord is transformed into a golden-tressed figure who shows little sign of having struggled for hours through heavy brush and marsh, and, although they were as physically imposing as the painting suggests, the Mohawk warriors had in fact largely adopted European clothing. Secord's brave effort came to symbolize in later years the Canadian determination to resist the American assault, and became part of the mythology of the war.

during his overnight stay at the Queenston home of James and Laura Secord sent Laura Secord off by foot on an arduous trek to warn FitzGibbon. She was found by Mohawk warriors – who knew Boerstler was coming and were laying an ambush – who took her to FitzGibbon. There the exhausted woman told an appreciative FitzGibbon what, in fact, he already knew.

The warriors laid the ambush well, in a heavily wooded area made sodden and dark by incessant rain. The warriors were commanded by Dominique Ducharme, and included a party from the Caughnawaga settlement near Montreal. Boerstler's column, accompanied by a train of supply wagons, blundered into the ambush, in which the Caughnawagas did the lion's share of the fighting. After a brief battle, FitzGibbon was able to use the Americans' fear of the warriors and the arrival of a party of redcoats who had marched down from Twelve Mile Creek, to convince Boerstler to surrender. It was a notable victory for the warriors, and it gave Vincent another success to add to Stoney Creek and Forty Mile Creek. Cautiously, he advanced his posts, until he found he was able to reoccupy Fort Erie, set up posts along the Niagara River cartway itself, and even send raiding parties across to the New York shore. Dearborn had gone to ground inside Fort George, and would not come out. The War Hawk and newly minted brigadier general, Peter B. Porter, raved:

> We have had an army at Fort George for two months past. . . . panic-struck, shut up and whipped in by a few hundred miserable savages, leaving the whole of this frontier, except the mile in extent which they occupy, exposed to the inroads and the depredations of the enemy.

Porter had every reason to be furious. Dearborn had managed to throw away every advantage gained, from the capture of York and the taking of the Niagara frontier to the pursuit of Vincent. With what Harrison was about to achieve on the Detroit frontier, Upper Canada was within a hair's breadth of conquest. Now the conquerors, at least on the Niagara frontier, were penned in their lair, awaiting the defenders' next move.

It was left to Isaac Chauncey's naval squadron, paired with an infantry force under the command of the fire-breathing Winfield Scott, to demonstrate any continuing energy in the American efforts on the Niagara front. Chauncey had arrived at Fort George in late July, anchoring in the rushing current to embark Scott's force, with a view to a landing at Burlington Bay and the seizure of Vincent's supplies.

The few troops left at York marched towards Burlington as Chauncey's sails were sighted, only to have Chauncey dodge entrapment of his force on the shore by re-embarking the few men landed and sailing up to York. The hapless capital endured another occupation on July 31, 1813, before Chauncey deposited Scott and his men back at Fort George.

A kind of quiet settled over the Niagara frontier as the drama of the war moved elsewhere. At sea, the powerful Royal Navy had been continuing to suffer scattered humiliations as American vessels won single-ship contests. This ended when HMS *Shannon*, 38 guns, took the unlucky USS *Chesapeake*, 38 guns, and towed her into Halifax. British vessels had begun to operate on Lake Champlain, south of Montreal, and American joy at repulsing an attempted naval bombardment of Burlington, Vermont, on June 13 was dimmed by the loss of two schooners, *Growler* and *Eagle*, which had been caught by British troops from Fort Lennox, Ile aux Noix, where the lake entered the Richelieu River, and had been forced to surrender.

THE SHANNON commanded by Cap.ᵗ BROKE engaging and capturing the CHESAPEAKE american Frigate, Cap.ᵗ LAWRENCE. in sight of Boston June 1.ˢᵗ 1813. his gallant action was terminated in 15 ᵐⁱⁿ cap.ᵗ Broke boarding at the head of a body of his crew. the american mounted 32pounders (the Shannon but 18) was 190 tons larger, and contained 110 more men than the British. cap.ᵗ Lawrence died of his wounds soon after she struck — a Subject we hope M.ʳ Maddison will not forget to mention the next meeting of Congress. Pub.ᵗ July 1813 by S. Knight M.ˢ Sweetings Alley.

On Lake Ontario, as the summer waned and fall approached, Chauncey and Yeo prepared their fleets to grapple with one another, each aware that a single disastrous defeat of his fleet might bring an end to the war – and his career. In the first week of August, the two rival fleets manoeuvred but never closed with one another off the mouth of the Niagara River. Chauncey finally departed for Sackets Harbor after the loss of four lesser vessels, two by capture and two – the schooners *Hamilton* and *Scourge* – sunk in minutes by a squall in the western part of the lake. Four weeks later the rival fleets met again, off York, and this

A composite view showing Chesapeake *at the moment she was devastated by* Shannon's *precisely aimed broadside, but with British colours flying already over the American. Philip Broke was severely wounded in the fight, and James Lawrence was killed, but not before crying out "Don't give up the ship!", a slogan that Perry flew on a flag at Put-In Bay in September of the same year, 1813.*

time Chauncey had the luck. In a brief exchange of gunfire, Chauncey's flag-ship, the *General Pike*, managed to damage Yeo's flagship, *Wolfe*. The *Wolfe* was saved from more serious damage when one of Yeo's officers, William Mulcaster, drove his vessel, *Royal George*, into position to screen the strug-gling *Wolfe*. In building seas and under threatening skies, Yeo's fleet ran off downwind to Burlington Bay to recover and repair. Chauncey pursued, and might have pressed in to complete the victory, but his caution took over: he was on a lee shore, and, with a planned major campaign now certain for the eastern end of the lake in a few weeks, he could afford no loss. He turned away from a relieved Yeo. The bemused soldiery on shore gave the name "Burlington Races" to the long chase.

The temporary American occupation of the Niagara frontier in the spring of 1813 had revealed disturbing divisions in Canadian society. The presence of so many farmers who were of American origin had been a worry to Brock, and remained one for the men who succeeded him. When Dearborn had taken Fort George and the frontier, and the evidence seemed clear that the United States was on the path to victory, many Canadians who in secret had wished for an American success were encouraged by events to come forward. And, as Brock feared, they came forward in surprising numbers, offering to Dearborn their "parole," or promise not to take part in the war. With some pleasure Dearborn wrote to the secretary of war that "a large majority are friendly to the United States and fixed in their hatred against the Government of Great Britain." If many Canadians were prepared to fight in the militia ranks in defence of the country, a sizeable number were not, and welcomed the prospect of American victory. To a degree this meant that Canadians were fighting what amounted to a civil war, and were being forced to make the same choices that Americans had made forty years earlier dur-ing their Revolution: loyalty to the new home, or adherence to the old.

The Canadians who threw in their lot with the United States found them-selves on thin ice when the American reverses at Stoney Creek and Beaver Dams suggested the war was not yet won. In some cases they took up arms, and parties of these "Canadian Volunteers" were raised by the Americans to do the work of patrol scouting, and to harass loyal subjects on many pretexts, including the settlement of old scores. This activity

(Above) His flagship Wolfe damaged,
Yeo and his squadron fled southwest ahead
of Chauncey in a long sailing pursuit
that watching British troops named the
"Burlington Races." Chauncey finally turned
away as he approached a dangerous lee shore,
and Wolfe surged into the shallow water at
Burlington Bay to take refuge and attempt
repairs.

Artist Peter Rindlisbacher's masterly depiction
of the September 1813 engagement between
Yeo and Chauncey on Lake Ontario (left). It
shows the moment when Chauncey's flagship
General Pike was prevented from destroying
Yeo's Wolfe. William Howe Mulcaster drove
his Royal George into place, sheltering
Wolfe, and engaged General Pike.

To The PATRIOTS OF THE Western District.

THE period being at hand which is to decide the fate of the province of Upper Canada, and the command of the Niagara frontier having devolved on me; I think proper to invite *The Old and Young PATRIOTS of the Western District,* to join my Brigade in defence of their Country and rights—Any number not exceeding one thousand will be accepted and organized immediately on their arrival at Lewiston, and officered by the choice of their men. As the movements of an army require secresy, objects in view cannot be particularly developed; but those who feel disposed to distinguish themselves and render services to their country, may be assured that something effectual ... two months, if not sooner discharged. And every thing shall be done to render their situation as comfortable as possible. I wish none to volunteer who may have any constitutional objections to cross the Niagara river. One thousand four hundred of my brigade, have already volunteered to cross the river, and go wherever they may be required; and six hundred of them are now doing duty at Fort George. I flatter myself that no other consideration need be urged, than a love of country, to excite the patriotism of the hardy yeomanry of the Western District.

Given at Head Quarters, Lewiston, Oct. 2d, 1813.

GEO. M'CLURE, Brig. Gen'l,
Commanding Niagara Frontier.

BUFFALO GAZETTE OFFICE, Saturday Evening, Oct. 2, 1813.

A recruiting broadside issued by George McClure, who had been given authority over the captured Canadian Niagara territory. The men he collected indulged in an orgy of looting and plunder before they abandoned the frontier in December, burning Newark as a last step. He thereby ignited a pattern of retribution that would leave the communities on both sides of the Niagara frontier in smoking ruins.

became particularly bitter along the Lake Erie coastline and in the Niagara Peninsula, where some hundred of these Volunteers, wearing green-and-white cockades, served under a former member of the Upper Canadian legislature, Joseph Willcocks. Under this man, and others such as Benajah Mallory, Canadian households experienced the nightmare of partisan raiding and looting, which became more uncontrolled when the United States's regular troops left the Niagara region for the fall campaign that was to come against Montreal, and an ill-disciplined force of three thousand New York militia took over the occupation of Newark, Fort George, and the trampled no-man's-land that the Niagara region had become. The militia was joined by Willcocks's turncoats and other lawless men from the United States, and leading this plunder-minded horde was General George McClure, who did nothing to protect the inhabitants from looting and abuse, and who had been prominent in the burning of public buildings at York. Once more, as in the Thames Valley a year earlier, the behaviour of those called in to bear arms for the United States in the early conquest of a cousin state proved to be the enemy of that cause, a reality that American leadership either failed to see, or saw no need to acknowledge. Loyalists were thus hardened in their resistance to the invaders, and recent American arrivals who had welcomed Dearborn's men were now dismayed at the actions of their former countrymen and began to regret that welcome. Before the year was out, McClure would commit an act that was barbaric and unnecessary, and which would bring the retaliatory torch to American homes and communities, hardening the remaining civilities of the war into a cold-eyed British and Canadian desire for revenge. The chance that Congress might win Canadian hearts was now gone; Canada would have to be won with blood and the bayonet.

The evident superiority of Chauncey's Lake Ontario fleet over Yeo's, which the Burlington Races appeared to confirm, was evidence of a deeper problem afflicting the British effort to maintain control of the two lower lakes, Erie and Ontario. The question of poor resources bedevilled Yeo at Kingston, for Sir George Prevost had made it clear that his greatest fear, still, was the classic thrust at the heart of Canada up the Champlain Valley. The Governor General was fighting a defensive, limited war that had

written off anything above Kingston as expendable and indefensible should a crisis come. Whether this was because of the severely limited means available to him, or because of his own timid nature, it lay like a cloud of restraint over the naval and military leadership in Canada. Those leaders were enjoined to fight a reactive war, meeting the American assault with only just enough force to blunt it, knowing that the initiative of a Brock or any action that risked resources would not be supported. Such was to be the fate of the overtasked Henry Procter at Fort Malden, and it transformed Yeo at Kingston into a cautious, hesitant man instead of a combative officer trained in the tradition of Horatio Nelson. Such a policy allowed the Americans to fight where they chose, recover, and fight again, without having the war carried to them. Critics of Prevost debated then, as they do now, whether his hesitant policies showed prudent practicality or a misuse of resources provided to him – a misuse that led to needless suffering on the part of the Canadian civilian population and put his government in a difficult bargaining position when negotiations eventually took place.

Kingston at the time of the War of 1812, seen from the site of Fort Henry and looking southwest. The Royal Navy dockyard in the centre of the picture was situated where the Royal Military College of Canada now stands.

A view to the south from Amherstburg, looking down the Detroit River towards Lake Erie in the distance.

With Prevost's hesitation hampering him at every turn, Yeo found himself having to match Chauncey on Lake Ontario, ship for ship, fleet for fleet, rather than seeking a psychological or strategic advantage over him. If there was no argument that Lake Ontario was the more important of the two lakes, Yeo still showed poor judgement in his failure to support the struggling British naval squadron on Lake Erie, on which Procter, Tecumseh, and the defenders of the Detroit frontier relied. When Yeo took over from the Provincial Marine at Kingston in 1813, he did not accept that his naval responsibilities for Lakes Champlain, Erie, and Ontario required him to spread his resources – carefully parcelled out by Prevost – equally on those waters. He did send off two competent officers, Daniel Pring to Ile aux Noix and Barclay to Amherstburg on Lake Erie. But the bulk of the men and matériel available to Yeo remained at Kingston, where he built over the next year and a half a remarkable squadron of carefully constructed warships, which Chauncey at Sackets Harbor was forced to match – albeit with workmanlike gun platforms almost crude in comparison with Yeo's Admiralty-pattern ships. Unlike Yeo, of course, Chauncey had the whole seaboard of the United States from which to draw men, skills, and resources, while Yeo had to have much shipped out from Britain. Yet the remarkable thing was that Yeo was able to obtain a great deal in the way of supplies, without giving away too much to Chauncey in that regard.

Where the difference lay in the two men – and this may not have been in Yeo's control – was in the attention Chauncey paid to the needs of the lake fleets besides his own and Yeo's comparative inattention.

If such a judgement is unfair to Yeo, the reality of meagre resources was very apparent to Procter, fighting his lonely little war on the Detroit frontier and waiting for William Henry Harrison's hammer blow to fall on him. When Robert Barclay arrived at Amherstburg in the spring of 1813 to build up a Lake Erie fleet, he found a respectable little squadron of five ships sitting at anchor off Fort Malden, with another vessel under construction, the largest of which was the nine-gun *Queen Charlotte*, which had performed creditably during the 1812 assault on Detroit. The crews of the Provincial Marine were also able enough as merchant seamen, but had neither the numbers nor the disciplined experience to operate the ships as fighting warships. Manning would be a constant problem for Barclay; he had arrived with only nineteen Royal Navy seamen, and, even if Sir George Prevost made weakly supportive noises to Procter, Roger Sheaffe's replacement in Upper Canada, Francis de Rottenburg, was not inclined to send infantry to Amherstburg to serve as marines. At the same time, Yeo could not, or would not, send more seamen. Procter and Barclay would have to get along with what they had.

As Barclay took his little ships to sea for the first time, wondering how he could turn the casual hands of the Provincial Marine into fighting seamen, the lake was still largely his. Chauncey had sent off Oliver Perry to Presque Isle with a hefty set of orders: build a squadron, wrest control of the lake from Barclay, and make possible Harrison's thunderclap descent on the Detroit frontier. Perry soon proved to be a productive leader, and he rapidly put together three workmanlike fighting vessels with keels laid for

Robert Barclay, a partially disabled Trafalgar veteran, struggled against the problems of inadequate equipment and untrained manpower to mount an effective British naval presence on Lake Erie.

two more. The release of the five schooners trapped under the guns of Fort Erie had provided more, and supplies were flowing up from Pittsburgh; Perry was contemplating a challenge to Barclay by high summer, if he could solve one problem of seamanship. He was building his fleet behind a sandbar that lay off Presque Isle, and which kept him in as much as it kept Barclay's ships out. The bar would be passable only if Perry stripped his ships of their guns, and Barclay was exploiting this, having set up a hovering blockade that would swoop in and cannonade Perry's unarmed ships if they tried to float over the bar.

Barclay's forward defence was admirable, and very much in the tradition of Nelsonian seamanship. But behind the walls of Fort Malden, Procter could look only with dismay at his small and diminishing resources. The augmentation of his garrison had been denied by de Rottenburg; Harrison was looming to the south; Barclay was keeping Perry's growing squadron bottled up, but there was no way of knowing for how long; and the severity of a hot, dry summer had reduced food supplies to the point where Procter faced being unable to feed his own people, Tecumseh's warriors and their families, and Barclay's seamen. Procter was doing his best, but by mid-July 1813 he had to watch Perry's fleet building with the dismay of a man who sees foul weather approaching but cannot seek shelter:

The detention of the force ordered here by the Commander of the Forces has prevented this district being in a state of security, which the destruction of the enemy's vessels at Presque Isle

Oliver Hazard Perry *by John Wesley Jarvis.* *Perry's victory over Robert Barclay at Put-In Bay in 1813 would be the result of determination, seamanship, and luck, and would give the United States its only thoroughly successful campaign of the war. Seen here in a captain's uniform of the United States Navy, Perry joined Harrison after his victory and would be present at the Battle of Moraviantown, narrowly escaping the loss of his horse. Not long after the war he died of fever in South America.*

would have effected – a service that might very easily have been completely effected a very short time since, but which, I apprehend, may now be attended with much difficulty. I should also have had it in my power to have supplied myself, at the enemy's expense, with provisions, of which we have not an adequate supply at present.

If Procter was a man facing a death sentence, he acted with commendable energy in trying to keep his opponents off balance as long as he could, to the limit of his character and ability. Brock's shoes were still hard to fill. Procter knew Harrison was amassing men both at Fort Meigs and on the Sandusky River, and he knew it was only a matter of time before Perry got out and challenged Barclay's lick-and-promise fleet. He was running out of food and time, and he had Tecumseh waiting expectantly for some sign that the redcoats had not given up. While Barclay still held nominal command of Lake Erie, Procter did what he could to carry the war to his enemy off the western end of Lake Erie.

It was Tecumseh who hatched the next scheme and, whatever Procter felt about its military sense, he acted on it, both out of a hope that some success might accrue from action rather than a hopeless inaction, and to keep faith with the warriors. Tecumseh's plan was to return again to the tough-but-tempting prize of Fort Meigs, on the Maumee, with a force of redcoats and warriors as before. But the plan now called for the British to arrive outside the fort and stage a believable mock battle that would convince the watching American garrison that a column marching to relieve the fort had been ambushed by warriors. It was hoped that this would lure the garrison out in rescue, and Procter's men would then pounce and secure a victory. It was based on the thin premise that Harrison would not know of his own troop movements, but Procter agreed.

On July 26, after a short voyage in Barclay's available ships and boats, including an undisturbed ascent of the Maumee, Procter and Tecumseh arrived again before Fort Meigs, with several hundred redcoats, perhaps a thousand warriors, and a few light guns. Duly, Tecumseh's warriors began a noisy sham battle in the woods outside the fort, the enthusiasm of which was literally dampened with the arrival of a tremendous rainstorm and the refusal of the garrison within the fort to move an inch, other than to peer imperturbably over their log ramparts at the sputtering skirmish. Clay, the post commander, remembered the rough handling his relief column had received at Tecumseh's hands and prudently stayed behind his walls. The gambit had failed, and on July 28 Procter called off the soggy effort and prepared to return to Fort Malden.

Tecumseh, however, had other ideas. Some kind of blow had to be struck against the Long Knives. To the east of Fort Meigs, on the Sandusky River, a short distance from where it empties into Lake Erie, a small American post named Fort Stephenson had been built. It was a modest structure of three blockhouses linked by a log stockade, lying behind a protective ditch. Its garrison was likely to be small, but it was in Harrison's domain. Tecumseh pressed Procter to try for its capture, and Procter agreed quickly; his personal inclination from the beginning had been to attack Fort Stephenson, but he had agreed to the Fort Meigs plan for Tecumseh's sake. The little force worked along the Lake Erie shore, and moved its boats up the Sandusky River to arrive in front of the fort on

The abortive attack on Fort Stephenson, launched by Procter after his failure to take Fort Meigs, was repelled by the steadiness of the fort's 160 defenders, who inflicted heavy losses on the assaulting redcoats.

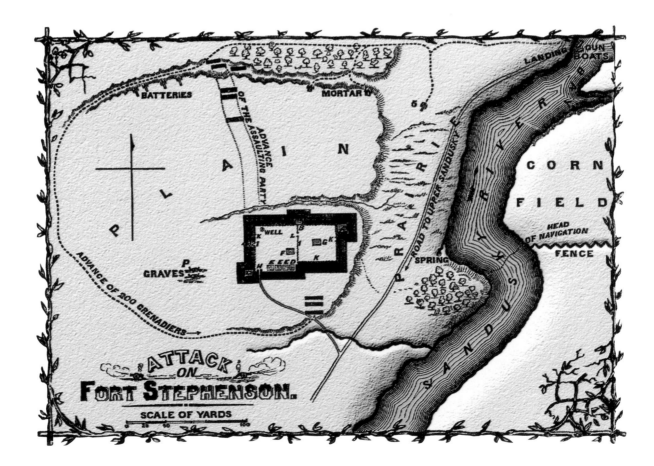

August 1. The post was commanded by a Major George Groghan, who had only 160 American regular infantry and one six-pounder gun with which to defend the place; he had received orders from Harrison to evacuate should Procter appear, but the British had arrived so unexpectedly that it was too late to flee. Rather than be cut to pieces on the run, Groghan prepared to fight as best he could.

Procter did not have the full force that had been at Fort Meigs, for Tecumseh had gone off with a large number of the warriors to range about the woods between Fort Meigs and Fort Stephenson. But he had his artillery, and he set up an emplacement and began a bombardment. The small field guns and mortars made little dint in the stout logs of the stockade, so Procter determined to simply rush his infantry at the place, led by the work-worn 41st Regiment.

In the waning afternoon sunlight, with the heavy white smoke of the day-long bombardment still lying low over the stump-strewn field before the fort, three columns of redcoats moved forward. Their glinting bayonets, their black cylindrical shakos, and the white crossbelting over the dusty red of their coats made an impressive sight as they came on over the dry ground, heading for the northwest corner of the stockade. Groghan held his fire until the British columns were less than a hundred feet away, then loosed an accurately aimed volley from his 160 muskets. The leading files of the 41st crumpled away under the hail of lead balls, and the warriors who had been trotting beside the columns faded back into the treeline, knowing suicide when they saw it. But the disciplined redcoats came on again, only to find that they could not scale the log palisade nor hack their way through it. At this range the American aim was deadly, and the repeated bravery of the attacks left heaps of dead and writhing wounded amid the sawdust and stumps. More than a hundred men of the 41st were killed, including their colonel. With nightfall, the admiring warriors stole out from the treeline and carried the wounded redcoats back to safety.

Now, receiving word that Harrison was approaching, Procter knew the attack was a failure. The shattered redcoats were got back to the boats and taken to Fort Malden, while the warriors went off to find Tecumseh; Groghan and his men breathed a sigh of relief. The futility of Procter's efforts was evident, even given the wasted bravery of his few, and diminishing, redcoats. The failed efforts against Fort Meigs and Fort Stephenson

Men of the 41st Regiment, depicted in uniforms that are slightly inaccurate – and far more pristine than would have been the case – struggle to hack their way into the northwest corner of the fort while under intense fire from within. Without proper scaling ladders, the regiment suffered many casualties, including that of their colonel, before Procter halted the useless slaughter and called them back to the boats.

had been possible only because of Barclay's control of Lake Erie. Now that was about to change as well, with disastrous results for Procter, Tecumseh, and the inhabitants of western Upper Canada.

At almost the same moment that Procter returned to Amherstburg with his bloodied little force, Robert Barclay's naval blockade of Perry inside the bar at Presque Isle suddenly evaporated. Perry was astonished to look out on July 30 and see no distant British sails. They would not return until August 4, before which the energetic Perry would accomplish much indeed. The reasons for Barclay's absence were never recorded, and it is hard to accept the folk

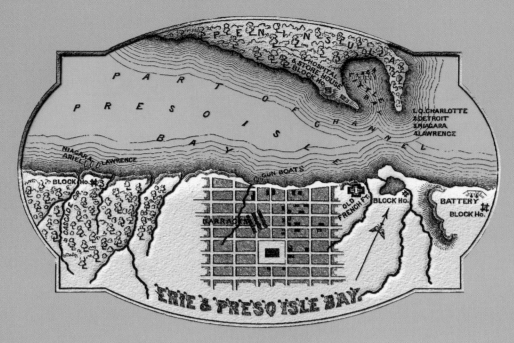

ERIE & PRESQ'ISLE BAY.

This plan of Presque Isle Bay, out of which Perry sailed to defeat Barclay, shows the positions of the captured British vessels at anchor following the battle.

Artist Peter Rindlisbacher presents with painstaking historical accuracy the look of the naval station at Amherstburg prior to Barclay's departure for his confrontation with Perry.

This artist's depiction of Barclay's flagship Detroit *suggests its size and general look, although the gunports would likely have not had the elaborate lids shown, and the ship's Red Ensign normally would have flown from the mizzen gaff rather than the head of the mizzen-mast.*

legend that Barclay sailed off with his squadron to escort an attractive widow from Amherstburg eastward along the lake, trusting to an onshore wind to keep Perry penned up. Nonetheless, when he sailed back to resume his station off Presque Isle, Perry was at sea on the lake with a squadron that outmatched his own.

Perry's feat in getting his vessels over the sandbar was an exercise in sea-manship. His two largest ships were the most difficult to manoeuvre. Freed from the fear of Barclay's ships, Perry solved the problem by using what were known as "camels." The ships were lightened of every possible bit of weight, particularly their guns, and then barges full of water were pulled alongside the ships' hulls and securely fastened on either side. The water in the barges was then pumped out, increasing their buoyancy and, in rising in the water, they lifted the hulls of the warships enough that they could scrape over the sandbar in four feet of water. A southerly wind helped lift the ships over, and within hours the brigs and schooners were riding at their anchors in deep water, feverishly loading aboard from lighters the guns, equipment, men, and supplies that had been taken off for the cross-ing. As soon as Perry was ready, he set his course westward along the Lake Erie coast, steering for the sheltered anchorages of Put-In Bay in the Bass Islands, which lay just off the mouth of the Sandusky River. There he would be in a position to assist Harrison's move against the Detroit frontier.

When Barclay tacked up the lake and saw that Perry was out, he realized that the balance of power had shifted within a few hours. Perry's squadron outmatched him in nearly every way. When the word was brought to Procter at Fort Malden, he knew that, with his thousand or so remaining troops, he stood little chance if Perry could embark Harrison's four thousand men and deposit them anywhere he chose. Supplies fell lower, and, with Perry on the lake, the supply schooners and bateaux beating up from Port Dover and Long Point were no longer safe from capture. It was with a certain des-peration that Procter pressed on Barclay a simple, if almost hopeless, plea: he must meet and destroy Perry's squadron.

To have a chance at beating Perry, Barclay knew he must have his new flag-ship, the small frigate *Detroit*, in his line of battle. The vessel was virtually complete, but because of the chronic denial of resources to the Detroit fron-tier, the guns meant for HMS *Detroit* were still at Kingston and had not been forwarded by Yeo. Barclay had nowhere near the experienced manpower that Perry had. In contrast to the well-trained, capable hands Perry had received from the blockaded Atlantic coast, Barclay had relatively few trained Royal Navy seamen. He had to make do with the surviving Provincial Marine men, Canadian volunteers, fur-trade employees, soldiers borrowed from Procter's garrison, and even a few of Tecumseh's warriors. *Detroit*

C·W·JEFFERYS

This C.W. Jefferys drawing dramatically illustrates the difficulty faced by Barclay's gunners, who had no "gun locks" to fire their assorted mix of guns, but had to use blank-loaded pistols instead. Thus hampered, they nonetheless fought heroically, reducing Perry's flagship to a ruin before the fortune and flow of the battle turned against them.

joined the squadron, sawdust and shavings still on her decks, but, without the guns still at Kingston, she had to be armed with any gun that could be made available from the ramparts of Fort Malden, many of which were decrepit and could only be fired by touching off a blank-loaded pistol at the vent.

Barclay had no illusions about what faced him, but he courageously put out into the lake on September 9, saluting Fort Malden as he was carried by the river current out into the warm waters of Lake Erie. He set canvas and steered southeast for the Bass Islands, his six vessels a brave sight on the lake, red commissioning pennants curling from the mainmast heads, the great Red Ensigns rippling on their gaffs like palette-knife swabs of colour against the September sky. After a quiet night on the lake, he sighted the Bass Islands and Perry's anchorage at Put-In Bay. In sight as well were the sails of Perry's nine vessels, standing out. The contest was about to take place, and there would be no graceful manoeu-vring and avoiding of action as on Lake Ontario. Each man had to win and shatter the other's force. There would be no turning away.

The ships drifted in light airs towards one another, neither force seeking anything other than to get alongside the ships of the enemy. Both the Royal Navy and the United States Navy were born of the same traditions of unflinching acceptance of action, and this day there would be a sadly heroic demonstration of that common characteristic. Barclay's guns had longer ranges; Perry's weapons were mostly short-ranging guns known as "carronades," that threw twice the broadside of Barclay's ships, and Perry steered for the British line with every use of the wind possible, trying to close the range.

The silence was shattered when Barclay's gunners on the *Detroit* and *Queen Charlotte* opened fire with their strange mix of guns. Strange mix or no, however, the cannonading inflicted tremendous damage on Perry's flagship, the *Lawrence*. The two squadrons drifted together in three clumps of vessels, blazing away now at one another in a continuous storm of fire that could be heard like distant summer thunder on the Canadian and American shores of the lake. The *Lawrence* lay close aboard the *Detroit*, the British and Canadian gunnery so furious that the American flagship had become an unmanage-able wreck. *Detroit* had beaten her first adversary, but at terrible cost: Barclay was seriously wounded, his first lieutenant had been killed, and a junior offi-cer was in command of the ship. The decks of both ships were slippery with blood, and between the thunderclaps of the guns could be heard the scream-ing of men who had been horribly mangled by flying splinters.

Perry had no intention of hauling down his personal flag, however. He had himself rowed over in a surviving ship's boat to the brig *Niagara*, Jesse Elliott's vessel, which was relatively untouched, and steered it in to renew the ghastly struggle. Shot and splinters filled the air, scything down men in heaps, screams mingling now with the hoarse, shouted orders and the tremendous concussions of the guns. Towering clouds of smoke roiled up around the ships and drifted slowly over the placid lake surface to leeward. Now *Queen Charlotte* had lost her captain and first lieutenant and, in

With their vessels showing the fearful damage caused by close action, the American and
British fleets pause after the surrender to bury casualties at sea. Treatment of Barclay
and his men by Perry's crews was considerate and respectful, with Perry personally tending
Barclay's wounds.

BURIAL SCENE, OF THE OFFICERS SLAIN, AT PERRY'S VICTORY ON LAKE ERIE, SEPT. 10th 1813.

In a solemn military ritual, crews of both fleets gather on shore to bury the slain American
and British officers. Perry supported Barclay through the ceremony.

After his flagship, the Lawrence, *had been badly mauled by Barclay, Perry refused to strike his colours, but shifted them by boat to the undamaged* Niagara. *Her commander, Jesse Elliott, had not yet brought her into action. This rendering, inaccurate as to sailors' clothing, nonetheless captures the drama of the moment, as Perry is rowed across.*

manoeuvring to meet Perry's renewed advance in *Niagara*, *Queen Charlotte* and *Detroit* ran afoul of each other and became hopelessly entangled.

Perry quickly steered *Niagara* between the four smaller British vessels, who were holding their own with their American counterparts, and fired shattering broadsides into them as he glided by. He closed on the tangled forms of *Detroit* and *Queen Charlotte*, and at nearly point-blank range swung *Niagara* broadside-to. The carronades punched round after round into the stricken British vessels, marksmen aloft in the tops adding to the slaughter, until the colours of both British vessels were finally hauled down. The battle was nearly over, with two of the smaller British craft now surrendering. The last two were captured as they tried to tack away and escape. It was a total victory for Perry, and as the smoke drifted away over the still, debris-littered surface of the lake, it carried with it British control of Lake Erie, and any hope Procter had of resisting Harrison.

Perry was as gallant in victory as he was determined in battle. He and his men gathered in the British and Canadian wounded and treated them with brotherly care and consideration. Perry personally tended Barclay, and supported him as both men stood at a burial of the dead of both sides ashore in the Bass Islands. It was a poignant moment of mutual respect and decency that said as much about the honour of the respective navies as it did about the character of the men involved. Perry also sent a note, written on the deck of the shot-torn *Niagara*, to William Henry Harrison, who was waiting in his headquarters a short distance from Fort Stephenson. It told Harrison his moment had come.

> We have met the enemy and they are ours; two ships, two brigs; one schooner and one sloop. Yours with great esteem and respect,
>
> O. H. Perry

It was September 12, 1813. On that same day, a morose Henry Procter at Fort Malden wrote to General de Rottenburg that it was no longer possible to hold the Detroit frontier, now that the lake route of his supply boats was in American hands. He intended to bake bread with whatever flour he had left, and then retire with his troops, baggage, and attendant civilians along the Thames River eastward. His goal was to reach Vincent at Burlington, which promised some safety, since Dearborn's men had pulled back into

Fort George. Procter began by sending overland the women and children, the baggage, the cattle, and the crowds of Canadian farming families, now refugees, who had no wish to wait for the American return. Bateaux kept pace along the river. But not only were the troops slow in getting away from the fort, there was another difficulty. Procter had not told Tecumseh.

When the news that Procter was preparing to abandon the Detroit frontier reached him, the warrior chieftain was thunderstruck. Procter had not spoken to him since Barclay had sailed, and Tecumseh had no knowledge of the scale of the defeat. Now warriors arrived at Tecumseh's lodge with reports of British preparations for flight. If there was one memory that burned in the warrior mind, it was the perceived betrayal of the Indian cause in the peace treaty signed with the Americans in 1783, and the

A somewhat gloating American cartoon published after the American victories on the Great Lakes, showing King George III being forced to make more ships for the "Yankeys" to capture.

visible betrayal of the defeated warriors after the Battle of Fallen Timbers in 1794, when the British post on the Maumee, the now-dismantled Fort Miami, shut its gates to the warriors fleeing the American army. Now Procter was preparing to withdraw in the face of a likely American invasion, and had not bothered to consult with Tecumseh. It mattered little to the Shawnee that Procter told no one else of his decision either, even his second-in-command at Fort Malden, Lieutenant Colonel Augustus Warburton. Tecumseh had staked his honour and personal reputation on arguing for the value of the Indian alliance with the British, and his arguments had convinced many tribesmen to relocate with their families to the Detroit frontier, trusting his word that the British would fight for an Indian homeland secure from the Long Knives. Now, that alliance and Tecumseh's reputation were both at risk. The encampments of the warriors were soon aflame with anger and recriminations, and through the Indian agent, Matthew Elliott, Tecumseh made it clear that Procter must speak with his warrior allies about this.

Finally, on September 18, Procter agreed. John Sugden, Tecumseh's meticulous biographer, recalls the words Tecumseh spoke in the council-house at that moment:

> You always told us you would never draw your foot off British ground. But now, Father, we see your drawing back, and we are sorry to see our Father doing so without seeing the enemy. We must compare our Father's conduct to a fat animal that carries its tail upon its back, but when affrighted, it drops between its legs and runs off.

Tecumseh argued that Procter should stand and fight. His fort was well built, if lacking Barclay's captured guns; he had more than two thousand British infantry and warriors and field artillery, and the Americans were nowhere in sight. If a defeat occurred, then was the time to retreat. Procter had not told Tecumseh of Barclay's complete defeat, nor made it clear how precarious the British felt their position to be. Tecumseh then electrified the listening warriors with a ringing declaration that was as humiliating to Procter as it was tragically prophetic for Tecumseh.

> Father! You have got the arms and ammunition which our Great Father sent for his red children. If you have an idea of going away, give

them to us, and you may go and welcome for us. Our lives are in the hand of the Great Spirit. We are determined to defend our lands, and if it is his will, we wish to leave our bones upon them.

Procter's decision to retreat was not an unreasonable one, but it seemed so to the furious and scornful warriors, because Procter had not told them the truth. Now he did, revealing the full catastrophe that had taken place on the lake, and it did not take long for Tecumseh to realize the threat facing Procter. Perry could cut off all supply and reinforcement efforts along Lake Erie from Burlington, and could also pass up the Detroit to choke off the Thames River mouth and the cart track that followed it eastward. Procter had scarcely enough flour and supplies left to feed his troops, let alone the warriors and their families, who were consuming more than a dozen cattle daily and thousands of pounds of flour. If Procter was to make a stand somewhere, where would it be?

Procter would have preferred to retire eastward all the way to Burlington, at the head of Lake Ontario. There he would be close to support, and Harrison, if in pursuit, would not be. But to do this would infuriate Tecumseh's warriors. Procter had already decided to withdraw partway up the Thames, and attempt to hold a position there. If he was defeated, the next move would be the withdrawal to Burlington. Of all this, Procter had told Tecumseh and the warriors nothing, and his silence was inexplicable, as was his bizarre refusal to inform all but a few immediate friends among his officer corps. He ended the meeting at the council-house by promising to give Tecumseh a reply in two days, but the preparations for withdrawal went on. After a grim period full of tense feelings, Procter finally called in Tecumseh to discuss what was intended. With Elliott interpreting, Procter revealed their own situation, Harrison's strength and likely moves, the lack of support from Prevost, and his own intentions, which were to retire along the Thames River and halt at a settlement called Chatham, where a fortified position would be built, and Harrison resisted. It took Tecumseh several hours of reasoning with the warriors, but eventually slightly more than a thousand of them, representing more than eleven different tribes, agreed to retreat with Procter and fight with him at Chatham.

The great evacuation got under way. Civilian families reluctantly abandoning their farms, Indian women and children carrying all their possessions, the troops trudging in weary resignation, cattle lowing as they were herded along, wagon axles squealing in the dust, the long column snaked north towards the mouth of the Thames. On September 27, the rearguard at Fort Malden spotted Perry's fleet inbound off the lake with Harrison's advance party on board. The thunderclap was about to strike; within hours, the first of Harrison's five thousand men were ashore and entering Fort Malden. It was a bitter moment for Tecumseh, watching at a distance, and he was almost the last man to turn away and begin the march up the Thames.

The trek went on, Procter vanishing on ahead in his personal carriage, while Tecumseh remained with Colonel Warburton and the slowly moving column. Now word came that the Americans had not just occupied the border but were in pursuit, and at that news the exasperated Warburton was all for facing about and fighting Harrison on the spot. But Tecumseh said no; Procter was ahead, and presumably was having a defensive position prepared at Chatham. The column should move on and fight there, as agreed.

When the column arrived at Chatham, however, Tecumseh and Warburton found that Procter had misled them. There were no prepared positions – nor was there any Procter. The despair and rage that threatened

With the defeat of Barclay, Procter determined to evacuate Fort Malden ahead of the expected attack by Harrison. Along with the garrison, local settlers, warriors, and their families began the trek to the mouth of the Thames River for the long march east to Burlington Heights.

to overcome Tecumseh did not break through; with enormous self-control he reasoned with Warburton until the latter agreed to make a stand at Moraviantown, a small cluster of log huts and cabins inhabited by missionized Indians a short distance farther up the river. Then Tecumseh turned back with a small party of warriors – many were taking their families and dissolving into the woods – and attempted to hold back Harrison's pursuit force of three thousand men.

It took only a brief skirmish to give the Shawnee a glimpse of the powerful and determined enemy who was coming on after them – or, more correctly, after *him*. If William Henry Harrison had a principal goal in mind as he pushed his army into Canada, even beyond the defeat of the British or the taking of Canadian lands, it was the destruction of cohesive Indian fighting power and resistance to the expansion of the United States. Tecumseh's elusive buckskin-clad figure represented that power more than anything else. As Procter seemed to collapse as a leader, the focus came to fall on Warburton, and on Tecumseh. It may have been that the Shawnee felt Fate closing in on him, for eyewitnesses recalled that he seemed lit by a serenity and purpose that affected all who were around him. He was everywhere, cajoling and encouraging the dusty, dispirited redcoats of the 41st

Procter's placement of his troops is shown on the right and the American advancing force is shown on the left. Procter's choice of position was not entirely indefensible, but his use of a loose, open formation, and the demoralized exhaustion of his troops, opened the door to an American victory.

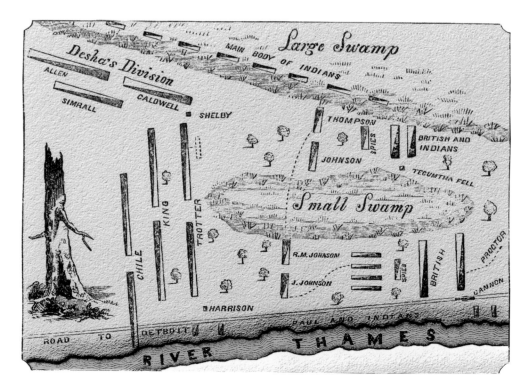

and the sombre, diminishing band of warriors, repeatedly being the last to retire when the Americans appeared in the distance.

But the pursuit was coming to a close; Harrison was overtaking the plodding column. As it approached Moraviantown, Procter appeared from ahead and ordered a halt there, since Tecumseh and Warburton had determined to fight. The Americans came on, smelling victory in the litter of equipment that lined the cart track and in the exhausted and demoralized little pickets of redcoats left behind by the column, who had been overrun in minutes. By October 5, Procter had formed the British infantry into an open line across the roadway before the little hamlet, the dispirited and hungry men confused as to what they were facing, or what Procter intended. They had only the cartridges in their personal cartridge pouches, and were arrayed in a thin formation two ranks deep, which Procter then weakened by drawing out every second file of men to make a reserve in the rear. Tecumseh spoke with Procter and said he would hold the right flank, putting his warriors into a swampy and wooded area that American horsemen would have difficulty entering. The afternoon dragged on, and for three hours Procter's infantry stood waiting, shuffling from one part of the line to another as Procter's whim took him. A great sense of dismay and foreboding filled the air, but Tecumseh seemed unaffected by it. Most of his warrior force had melted away, but he moved among his remaining loyal followers, encouraging them, and then, even though he spoke little English, he did the same along the weary line of British infantry. Every soldier who saw him remembered his passage. Tecumseh came at last to Procter, who, in so many ways, had not lived up to the Shawnee's expectations. Despite this, he encouraged him, saying, "Father, have a big heart!"

The attack came at about four o'clock. The large American force appeared, and in the lead was not the infantry, but the one thousand tough and capable mounted Kentuckians of Richard Johnson. Johnson's men formed into four columns and then galloped at the waiting British, who stood in open formation, rather than shoulder-to-shoulder. As the Kentuckians thundered in, Procter's men fired one volley,

Like William Henry Harrison, Richard Johnson, who led the Kentuckians against Procter's line, used his victory to support later political ambitions.

Remember the River Raisin! *Johnson's mounted Kentuckians, skilled in the use of weapons on horseback, thunder down on Procter's loosely formed line, overwhelming the redcoats in a few minutes.*

then another. Then it was over, the redcoat line shattered in several wild moments by the charge, most of the British infantry surrendering as the horses stamped and wheeled around them, the Kentuckians' tomahawk blades flashing down or flintlocks, held expertly with one hand, blazing at point-blank range. More than forty redcoats went down in that wild, dusty clash, with barely more than one Kentuckian a casualty. Procter bolted from the field moments before capture threatened, and abandoned his men to their fate.

The column of riders that galloped at the position held by Tecumseh's warriors met with a very different reception. At the last minute, the Indians delivered a brutal volley that brought down horses and men in tumbling, smoke-wreathed chaos, the whinnying of the horses keening high over the bang of the flintlocks and the curses of the riders. The desperate fury of the warrior resistance pushed the Americans back, but they rallied and came on again into the swampy woodland, the struggle now a hand-to-hand fight

An inaccurate depiction of the death of Tecumseh, done in 1833 to support the campaign of Richard Johnson to secure the vice-presidential nomination. Although Johnson is shown firing the fatal shot, Tecumseh's actual killer is unknown.

for survival for each man. Somewhere in the battle Tecumseh's voice could be heard, and men spoke afterwards of seeing him in the thick of the combat. But then a cry went up through the warriors. The Shawnee had fallen. The warriors paused, then melted back. Where a moment earlier they had grappled with the Long Knives, now they were gone. The Americans had the field, and Harrison had defeated not only Procter in a humiliating rout, but had at last smashed the heartbeat of the Indian resistance in the Old Northwest.

It was the end of one people's dream, and the success of another's. And it opened the Canadas to the very real peril of conquest.

Tecumseh had fallen, as Harrison had hoped he would. But even in death he inspired respect from foe as well as friend. One American recalled:

> Tecumseh is certainly killed. I saw him with my own eyes. It was the first time I had seen this celebrated chief. There was something so majestic, so dignified, and yet so mild in his countenance, as he lay stretched on his back . . . that while gazing on him in admiration and pity, I forgot he was a savage.

An imaginary representation of Tecumseh's last moments, this sculpture by F. A. Ferdinand Pettrich bears little resemblance to the probable appearance of Tecumseh, or his manner of dress; what it does represent is the degree of admiration for Tecumseh and the cause he espoused, which became – and remains – a powerful cultural and historical force.

The epilogue of the struggle was a sad one. Tecumseh died as a martyr to his cause, and with him died the last of the real Native conflict with the Long Knives in the Ohio–Wabash valleys, and onward to Lake Michigan. With him, too, died any serious British pretense to control the western part of Lower Canada for the rest of the war. Harrison, content with his victory, retired to the frontier, and the theatre of war shifted farther east, to Lake Ontario

and down the St. Lawrence River. The British still held sway in the north, on Lake Huron and at Mackinac, but Harrison had knocked over one of the three pillars of Canadian defence. If an American attack down the

St. Lawrence and up the Richelieu River Valley were to knock out the second, at Quebec, then the third – Vincent's command at Burlington, and the Niagara Peninsula, save for occupied Fort George, and York – would fall of its own accord. As Procter, the remains of his redcoats, and remnants of Tecumseh's people trekked wearily into Burlington, victory was tantalizingly within the grasp of the United States, and it had been put there by two men whose determination and competence had swept away the shame of Hull: Oliver Hazard Perry and William Henry Harrison. For Procter, court martial and condemnation awaited. As for Tecumseh, his death would bring a sense of loss and sadness as powerful as that produced by the loss of Brock – which was completely appropriate. Both men had shone as beacons of encouragement, as leaders; now the war had taken them both.

Sir George Prevost at Quebec now issued an order that would have capped Harrison's victory with a gift. He sent instructions to de Rottenburg to evacuate *all* of Upper Canada – Burlington, York, the Niagara frontier, all of it – and retire to Kingston. Prevost had convinced himself that prudence required him to hand over virtually all of Canada but the St. Lawrence Valley to the United States. General John Vincent at Burlington considered the order. He also considered what would be lost if he obeyed. The stores and supplies at Burlington would be forfeited and, with Chauncey's powerful presence on Lake Ontario, boats and vessels transporting men, goods, and likely refugees eastward to Kingston would be easy prey. Vincent decided to remain at Burlington, although he would have to pull in all his outposts and patrols, leaving the Niagara Peninsula fully open to months of looting and pillage at the hands of McClure's brutal militia and Willcocks's Canadian turncoats. In making this decision, however, Vincent kept alive the idea, and the reality, of Upper Canada – and ultimately the future Canada itself. Tecumseh might have left his bones on the earth he fought for; John Vincent's disobedience ensured that some part of what the Shawnee had died for would survive.

"And hold the enemy in check"

THE ST. LAWRENCE HEARTLAND DEFENDED

*A*S THE FALL LEAVES DEEPENED into gold once again, the United States secretary of war had reason to be optimistic. William Henry Harrison had smashed warrior power in the Old Northwest, redeemed the stain of Hull's surrender, and taken all of Upper Canada west of Lake Ontario, even though it was beyond his resources to effectively occupy it. If the British still had the upper hand in the remote northern or prairie posts, Lake Erie was now an American body of water, and Chauncey was at least as much master of Lake Ontario as Yeo. The British had not packed up and retreated to Kingston as Prevost had hoped, but York was a helpless little village, and the British forces near Niagara were bottled up at Burlington, allowing American occupation of the Niagara frontier. All that remained for the Americans, besides wondering what to do about the stubborn John Vincent, was to assault the final pillar of Canadian defence: to travel down the St. Lawrence to Montreal, and even possibly to Quebec itself. If the fall of 1813 offered anything to Secretary of War John Armstrong, it was the opportunity to seize everything from Montreal upriver, thus isolating posts at Kingston and Burlington and trapping Prevost in the Quebec remnants of his colony.

To make this all happen, Armstrong had determined to replace the corpulent and blundering Dearborn with an officer of dash and competence. But in doing so, he got no Harrison or Winfield Scott. James Wilkinson, a politically connected and shrewdly corrupt Revolutionary War veteran now in charge at New Orleans received the army's command, and the question was going to be whether the opportunity for achievement of the United States war aims against a wounded and reeling Canada would be safe in his hands.

At Quebec, Prevost was acutely aware that Armstrong was planning the eastern movement against him. He had several thousand regular infantry, including his well-trained but sparse Canadians in regiments such as the Voltigeurs and the Canadian Fencibles, and a large-if-untested militia drawn from the French-speaking settlements of Lower Canada, which seemed to him a "mere posse."

Once James Wilkinson arrived on the northern frontier on August 12, it was soon clear that the Americans planned some kind of concentrated movement involving the large force Dearborn had kept – but not used – at Sackets Harbor. It would now be enhanced by the American troops on the Niagara frontier, and the large army Dearborn had built up at Burlington, Vermont, supported by advanced posts at Swanton, Vermont, and at

James Wilkinson's appointment to command the northern campaign against Canada in 1813 guaranteed the likelihood of American failure. Corrupt, and more adept at political manoeuvring than competent leadership, he proved incapable of success, even though he was handed the greatest opportunity for the conquest of Canada that the United States would see in the war.

Plattsburg and Champlain, New York. Armstrong had, therefore, a strong army threatening the upper St. Lawrence, supported by the naval squadron of Isaac Chauncey, and an equally strong force on Lake Champlain, supported by the small United States Navy flotilla of Commodore Thomas Macdonough based at Burlington, Vermont. Wilkinson was at last installed in upper New York state.

Wade Hampton was a Carolina planter and land-speculator, appointed to command the Champlain Valley wing of the 1813 invasion of Canada on the basis of his Revolutionary War service and political connections. He despised Wilkinson, under whom he was expected to serve, and may have turned away from a victory over de Salaberry's determined little force at Chateauguay at least partly out of fear he would suffer a loss that would allow Wilkinson to remove and discredit him. The visceral enmity between the two men was a contributing factor to the collapse of the American campaign of 1813.

To complement Wilkinson, Armstrong appointed an equally political choice to command the army on Lake Champlain, in the person of Carolinian planter Wade Hampton. If the weapon aimed at the heart of Canada was an awesome one, the two hands on its hilt represented an unfortunate choice for the United States. Wilkinson had been involved in the cabal that had tried to undermine George Washington during the

Thomas Macdonough's deep religious convictions were matched with a competence and energy as a naval officer that rivalled Perry's. Commanding the American naval forces on Lake Champlain, he built them into an effective squadron, which he handled well in the bloody and conclusive 1814 victory off Plattsburg that ended Sir George Prevost's invasion attempt.

Revolution, had been accused of being in the secret pay of the Spanish, and had little to recommend him in the way of military rather than political prowess. Hampton, for his part, was a frontier planter and land speculator whose principal characteristic was an abiding hatred of Wilkinson, with whom he was meant to act in concert. On receiving his appointment, Hampton declared to Armstrong that he would not be subservient to Wilkinson, whatever the secretary of war ordered, and it took careful letters from Armstrong to make the difficult relationship work.

The success in the war so far had depended on the reliance of the land forces on the control of adjacent waters by supporting flotillas – a sound enough principle, provided it did not become the only operational imperative. Wilkinson knew that Kingston was well defended, and, although it had a protecting naval presence in the form of Yeo's squadron, that naval strength was matched by Chauncey's. Wade Hampton might have felt more secure on Lake Champlain, since until just prior to his arrival there, Lake Champlain was an indisputably American body of water – as Lake Erie was about to become. The small American squadron at Burlington, Vermont, supported by a shipyard farther south on Otter Creek, had been unchallenged on the lake, and its very competent commander, Thomas Macdonough, moved about it with ease. But events in midsummer shifted that balance, if only for a short time.

Macdonough's force featured two schooners, the *Growler* and the *Eagle*. To counter these and Macdonough's other vessels, the British had only three clumsy barges at Ile aux Noix, armed with one six-pounder gun in each bow. They were Provincial Marine vessels, and Sir James Yeo at Kingston had sent off Lieutenant Daniel Pring to take charge of them. On

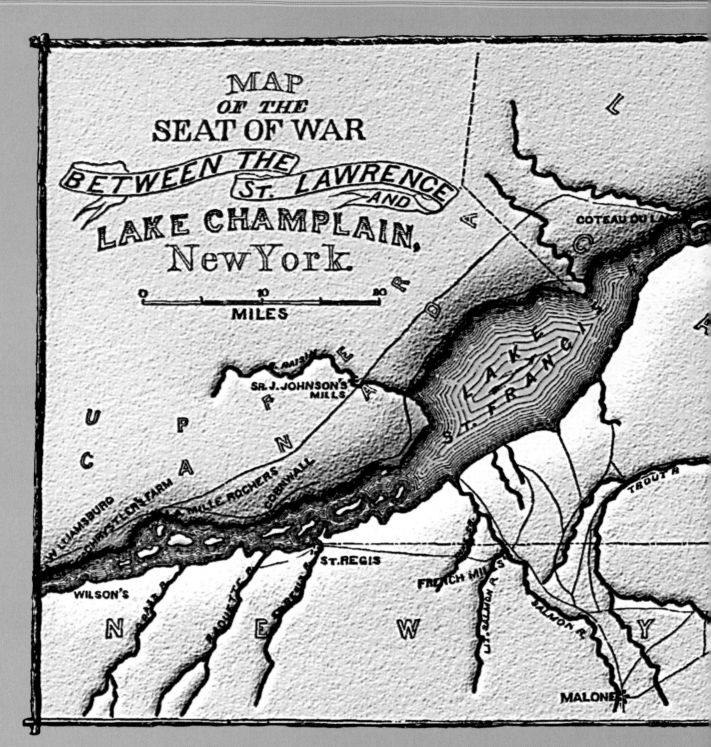

MAP
OF THE
SEAT OF WAR
BETWEEN THE ST. LAWRENCE AND
LAKE CHAMPLAIN,
New York

0   10   20
MILES

COTEAU DU LA

LAKE ST. FRANCIS

R. RAISIN

SR. J. JOHNSON'S MILLS

UPPER CANADA

TROUT R.

W. LIAMSBURG

CHRYSTLER'S FARM

MILLE ROCHERS

CORNWALL

WILSON'S

RAQUETTE R.

ST. REGIS

FRENCH MILLS

LT. SALMON R.

SALMON R.

MALONE

N   E   W   Y

Scene of the greatest invasion threat Canada faced during the war, in the fall of 1813.
Wilkinson, descending the St. Lawrence, was meant to rendezvous with Hampton, who was
descending the Chateauguay. The combined American army of over 12,000 men would have
Montreal within its reach when stopped by the defeats at Chateauguay and Crysler's Farm.

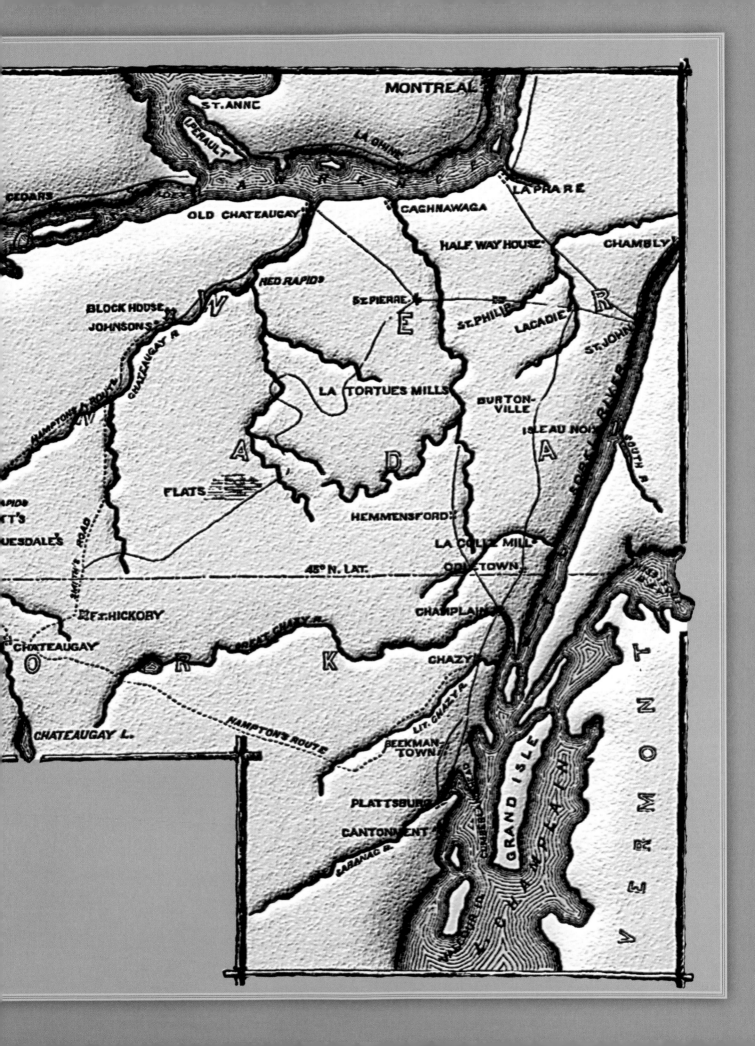

his arrival, however, Pring was to find his little command had been materially increased by the initiatives of the garrison commander at Ile aux Noix, Major George Taylor, who had managed to capture the two American schooners.

The loss of *Growler* and *Eagle* had come about partly by bad luck and a degree of rash behaviour by the American captains. Macdonough had sent the two schooners – each of which carried eleven small guns – on an exploratory voyage at the beginning of July. They were to move along the verdant shores of the lake and scout the British activity at Ile aux Noix. Taylor, however, was warned by a sentry of the schooners' approach, and he reacted quickly. The gunboat barges were manned, and soldiery packed into whatever bateaux were at hand. Taylor kept them well hidden until the schooners had worked their way into the river near the island, where turning would be difficult. Then he launched the boats at them, and in a hail of musket fire and splintering rounds from the barges' six-pounders the schooner captains hauled down their colours.

When Taylor sent off word to Montreal, where Roger Sheaffe had been commanding since his transfer from the Upper Canadian theatre, Sheaffe viewed the capture as a chance to strike, in some kind of unbalancing forward defence, at Wade Hampton's army, which was massing at Burlington. The cautious Prevost uncharacteristically agreed, but the Royal Navy commander at Quebec had neither officers nor men to spare for Taylor's boats. At that point, by pure chance, the British frigate *Wasp* arrived at Quebec, under the command of Thomas Everard.

Everard was more than anxious to get a taste of the war on fresh water, even though he was due to sail again in two weeks. Very quickly he was given permission to take a party of officers and men to Ile aux Noix – carrying with them the surprised and pleased Lieutenant Pring, who had just arrived from Kingston – and a striking force of British and Canadian infantry and artillery, under the command of Lieutenant Colonel John Murray. Everard found himself with orders to get to Ile aux Noix, render the captured schooners and bateaux fit to sail, cram the assault force into them, sail off down the lake, and be as upsetting to Wade Hampton's force as possible. Sheaffe was able to tell Everard and Murray that the staging base at Plattsburg, on the lake's west shore, was devoid of troops or ships, and that the newly arrived Wade Hampton had his four to five thousand men encamped in and around Burlington, Vermont. Macdonough's fleet was at Burlington as well, working up the replacement schooners for *Growler* and *Eagle*, which now sailed under the Red Ensign with the names *Broke* and *Shannon*. Everard and his army colleague were ordered to focus their attacks on Plattsburg and Burlington, do what they could to disperse troops and sink ships, burn public buildings – another legacy of Dearborn at York – and get back in time to return Everard and his men to *Wasp* by their sailing date.

On July 29, with the sun shining pleasantly on the peaks of the Adirondacks to the west, and the Green Mountains of Vermont to the east, the flotilla sailed off down the lake, the sea-going Everard marvelling at the novelty of sailing on his supply of drinking water. The flotilla kept to the west, or New York, shore, where Murray sent in a small party to the town of Chazy. They damaged public buildings but did not disturb the astonished population unduly before the flotilla moved languidly on, rounding Cumberland Head on July 31 and standing in to Plattsburg. The unprepared local militia took to its heels, leaving Murray's men to wander about for twelve hours, making off with anything military they could find and setting fire to a few military buildings. After a pause at Cumberland Head, Everard steered off to the southeast for Burlington.

At Burlington, Vermont, the United States Navy squadron was not in a state to sail and engage Everard as much as the intense and capable commander, Thomas Macdonough, might have wished. His crews were not up to strength, and the anchorage was crowded with schooners and scows that had put in for shelter on Everard's slow approach. Hampton's army brought into action a battery of guns situated on high land at the north end of the long, curving harbour, banging away enthusiastically if ineffectually at Everard's ships. Everard stood off and exchanged several long-range shots with the American battery, also firing at Macdonough's squadron, while he debated the wisdom of a landing. His ships and bateaux were crowded with almost a thousand willing infantry, but Everard prudently avoided stepping into the bear's den, sailing off instead for Shelburne Bay and several other communities farther south, while capturing some lake schooners and their cargoes. Content with his experience – and having swept the upper lake of virtually anything afloat – Everard tacked the force back to Ile aux Noix, suffering no casualties beyond a few deserters, and carrying back to *Wasp* much material for dinner conversation. Pring was left to take care of the squadron, albeit without Everard's men and the additional troops Murray had brought. It was an adventure for Everard, but accomplished little towards reducing Hampton's or Macdonough's capability. The next major visit of the Royal Navy to Lake Champlain would receive a very different sort of welcome.

Two weeks or so later a mountainous coachload of baggage and the reluctant figure of James Wilkinson arrived at windy Sackets Harbor. Wilkinson had finally accepted what Armstrong insisted the great fall campaign against Lower Canada would comprise. There was hope that Harrison would be successful on the Detroit frontier, and all troops that could be spared from Niagara would be assembled at Sackets Harbor. Wilkinson would act, as planned, in concert with Wade Hampton, in spite of the poisonous ill will that existed between the men, and Hampton's refusal to be considered the subordinate partner. Armstrong finally moved personally to Sackets Harbor to ensure the plan's success, but there were worries: it was not until Harrison's success on the Thames that Wilkinson would cease to fret about the Niagara frontier and leave it to the mercies of McClure's looters; and Yeo was still unbeaten in the strongly fortified and garrisoned town of Kingston. After Wilkinson made a last attempt to limit the plan to an attack on Kingston, he gave in and agreed to do what Armstrong wanted. Wilkinson would embark his troops and make as if to assault Kingston. Then he would turn downriver and descend the St. Lawrence rapidly towards Montreal. Meanwhile, Hampton would cross to Plattsburg from Burlington, Vermont, and march north to meet Wilkinson outside Montreal, after which the joint armies would assault the city. Armstrong had presented his plan to President Madison on July 23, 1813, and had received his approval. It promised to be the master stroke of the war.

An American infantryman of the 1813 campaign, as he might have appeared at Chateauguay as part of Wade Hampton's army. By October, the thin summer uniforms would be threadbare, and both at Chateauguay and on the St. Lawrence the American troops suffered severely from exposure.

At Burlington, Vermont, Wade Hampton now had a substantial force of mostly regulars of the United States Army, with slightly more than 5,000 infantry, 180 cavalry, and an artillery battery of "eight 6 pounders, one 12, and one howitzer, tolerably found." Thomas Macdonough's supporting Lake Champlain squadron consisted now of five schooner and sloop rig vessels, two row galleys, and a unique little steamboat, which Macdonough was readying, along with impressed civilian schooners, to transfer Hampton to Plattsburg. With Wilkinson's force at Sackets expected to reach seven thousand men, Armstrong was aiming a powerful weapon at Canada.

The agreed start date for the great, two-pronged assault on Montreal was to be September 25, and Hampton was to begin it at Plattsburg. Accordingly, Macdonough began to move him over on September 8, watching carefully to the north for British sails. His concern was unnecessary; Yeo's parsimony had left Pring with too few men to have brought out his squadron and bothered the convoys, which had the lake to themselves for the ten tedious days it took to transfer the army to Plattsburg. By September 18 Hampton was ready to march, and the next day the long column of men, horses, and wagons began to tramp dustily north in the hot September sunshine. Within a day, the first units crossed the border, surprising a British picket at Odelltown. But the great army did not stay there. Problems with Hampton's supply system – "a want of management in the system of the army," as one participant put it – were

Infantry officer, northern campaign of 1813. Possibly an officer of the New York State militia, some of whom did cross into Canada with Hampton.

already putting the march north at risk. Hampton had to contend as well with a lack of water. Local brooks had all gone dry in the intense heat, and provided no fresh water for either troops or horses. Hampton called his officers to a council of war, and they recommended marching west some seventy miles to the American hamlet of Chateauguay Four Corners, on the upper reaches of the Chateauguay River just below the Canadian border. There, they hoped they would have water and would be in a position to descend the river valley to meet Wilkinson before Montreal, or march northwest for an earlier junction.

The seventy-mile march proved a great strain on the ill-prepared army – one officer complained of being "compelled to abandon clothing and other things essentially necessary to preserve the body in health" – and when Hampton arrived at Four Corners on September 25 his supply system required much attention.

There was, however, a mixed blessing awaiting him in the despatches that now arrived from Sackets Harbor. Wilkinson had fallen ill, and the campaign would have to wait until his recovery, which was unpredictable. Hampton busied himself improving the cart track to Plattsburg and bringing up the consistently inadequate supplies. The weather had now turned from scorching late-summer heat to a cold, rainy fall, and Hampton's men had only their summer uniforms. Huddled in their rows of huts, they began to fall ill. They also now faced the threat of attack themselves.

Five days after the army had arrived at Four Corners, Canadians and warriors of the Indian Department had burst out of the dark pine woods and made a whooping ambush on several of Hampton's outlying pickets. Colonel Robert Purdy of the 4th United States Infantry Regiment recorded his impressions:

An enlisted man of United States Army artillery, which was present at Chateauguay and at Crysler's Farm in 1813. The artilleryman would sling his musket while serving as a member of a gun crew.

[The attack] had a bad effect on the morale of the army, the soldiers contracting an absurd dread of a foe who, though despicable in numbers, was unseen and unsleeping. The men shrank from sentry duty, and not a night passed without dropping shots from the woods. To this natural fear was added discomfort. No new clothing was issued, and the cotton uniforms for summer wear, now threadbare and ragged, were poor protection against the white frosts and rains of the fall. Food had to be hauled from Plattsburg, keeping 400 wagons, drawn by 1,000 oxen constantly on the road, so the supply was subject to the weather and often short.

The Canadian Voltigeurs were well-trained in the light-infantry tactics that suited forest warfare in Canada. For the most part, the British relied on their own regular regiments when confronting the United States Army in open-field, formal battles such as Crysler's Farm, using the Canadians as auxiliary troops.

The "unseen and unsleeping enemy" that had attacked Hampton's encampment sentries on October 1 was part of the relatively thin defence line, under the command of Major General Richard Stovin, which was spread out in a semi-circle through the countryside below Montreal. This line consisted in its advanced components almost entirely of Canadian troops, for the most part French-speaking. These were formed in regiments of regulars such as the grey-clad Voltigeurs, the red-coated Canadian Fencibles, and militia companies that had been selected to be trained up to regular standards – and thus were titled the Lower Canada Select Embodied Militia. There were also many companies of relatively untrained but numerous "sedentary" militia. There were as well Indian warriors, including Caughnawaga men who had won the fight at Beaver Dams. Stovin's strength lay in his access to the large and settled population of

Lower Canada, available and willing to fight in defence of their farms and villages. His weakness lay in the questionable ability of this defence to withstand the assault of an army of five thousand infantry, cavalry, and artillery. In reserve close to Montreal, Sheaffe kept back his final line of defence, relatively tiny numbers of British regulars.

As the attack on Hampton's camp demonstrated, the Canadians and their warrior allies did not intend to wait for Hampton to come to them. The initiative in this instance came in the form of the burly, ebullient French Canadian officer who commanded the Voltigeurs, a regiment he had raised from the Lower Canadian population. Charles-Michel d'Irumberry de Salaberry was the son of a Canadian seigneur, who had served in the British Army's 60th Regiment of Foot in the Caribbean and elsewhere, and was one of four brothers in British military service. Only Charles had survived the fighting, and he had served in the garrison in Ireland before being recalled to Canada.

In Canada he served as aide-de-camp to de Rottenburg until he was called on to form the Voltigeurs, or, to give them their proper title, the Provincial Corps of Light Infantry. The light-infantry tactics in which he trained them suited the marksmanship and woods sense of the young men he recruited, and by 1813 the Voltigeurs, in their grey uniforms with black bearskin caps, had become a formidable body of light troops that fought best alongside warriors in the stalk-and-strike war of the forest gloom. It had been de Salaberry who had launched the October 1 attack, using about a hundred warriors, two companies of the Voltigeurs, and the light-infantry company of the Canadian Fencibles, which was a mixed English and French unit comfortable in both languages.

Losses on both sides in the short exchange were light, the greatest impact being the fear of the warriors in the minds of Hampton's men. It was during his retirement back along the cart road beside the Chateauguay River that de Salaberry noted a series of ravines that ran into the river near the present hamlet of Allan's Corners, Quebec. It was here, de Salaberry believed, that a small force could set up a defensive position against Hampton's column. De Salaberry was aware that Hampton faced the alternative of moving west to the St. Lawrence or north towards Montreal. In the latter event, the Canadian knew where he would make his stand, should the choice be his.

Hampton undertook one diversionary raid in the hope of drawing off

*Charles-Michel
d'Irumberry de Salaberry.
De Salaberry's success
in raising the Canadian
Voltigeurs, and his effective defence, supported by
"Red George" Macdonnell,
which turned back the
Americans at Chateauguay,
make him one of the most
significant Canadian
figures of the war.*

some of Montreal's defenders. He sent orders back to Colonel Isaac Clark, the garrison commander at Burlington, Vermont, to send out a raiding party to Missisquoi Bay, at the Canadian end of Lake Champlain. On October 11, Clark's force of two hundred militiamen pounced on the small village of Philipsburg and captured the local militia detachment, who found themselves marched off to temporary captivity in Boston. Clark was also chagrined to find a stockpile of stores recently delivered to

Missisquoi Bay by enterprising Vermonters, who were making a respectable income supplying Sheaffe's army. Efforts to stop this trade by patrols of American dragoons out of Swanton and Burlington were themselves disrupted by raids of Canadian light troops, who apparently penetrated even as far south as Burlington to prevent such policing.

Beyond ordering Clark's incursion, Hampton did little else but await orders. He was deeply suspicious of Wilkinson and determined not to be caught in a debâcle that Wilkinson would blame on him. Messages and despatches were exchanged and, in the porous intelligence environment shared by both sides, the real target of Montreal was soon known by all, including Prevost. He had returned to Montreal at the end of September, and ordered troops east out of Kingston to help Sheaffe. The only question now was when the great enterprise would commence, not if.

Notice finally arrived in a letter from Armstrong at Sackets Harbor to Hampton, written on October 16. It reached Hampton's camp on October 18, and it informed Hampton that Wilkinson had finally struggled out of his sick bed and planned to set off almost immediately with his horde in an armada of boats down the St. Lawrence. Hampton was ordered to advance to the mouth of the Chateauguay River "or other point which shall favour our junction, and hold the enemy in check."

It was a clear enough order, and Hampton's way ahead was at first glance not a difficult one. There was a cart track which ran from Four Corners virtually the entire length of the river, and Hampton expected bridges to be torn up and impediments felled; neither prospect presented anything more than a potential annoyance. The forces awaiting him were assumed to be militia – he did not know that the first defended position would

The 2nd Regiment of United States Light Dragoons, cavalry who would dismount and fight as infantry, were the advance scouts for Hampton's army as it approached the Chateauguay and de Salaberry's waiting force.

be that of de Salaberry – and his stay at Four Corners had allowed him to improve if not rectify his supply and provisioning situation. After several days of readying, the army moved north into Canada on the morning of October 21, 1813. Left behind were 1,500 militia who flatly refused to cross, and who were assigned to guard the supply route to Plattsburg.

As soon as Hampton crossed the border, his lead units began to be sniped at by parties of warriors, fleeting will-o'-the-wisps visible in the shadows below the towering white pines. His scouts reported back to him that a section of the rutted roadway through these heavy woods, leading to more open country downriver, was "blocked up with felled timber, [and] was a serious impediment to the arduous task of opening a road for the artillery and stores." The cart track entered cleared land at the junction of the Outardes and Chateauguay rivers, at the farm of a man called Spears. A small detachment of local sedentary militia and about ten warriors occupied a rough blockhouse at the site. While Hampton busied his main body of troops in hacking aside the obstacles on the main road, he sent ahead his second-in-command, Brigadier General George Izard, with a column of light infantry and one line regiment to cut through the deep woods and take the Spears post, there to wait until the main army came up.

Izard was a competent officer, and the scouts led the Americans accurately through the forest gloom to Spears's. The column appeared unexpectedly out of the trees at about 4:00 p.m. on October 21, just as the militia and Indians were preparing dinner. There was a brief exchange of musketry and, before the brief defence was crushed, one man of the picket was sent off at a run to warn the officer commanding the pickets along the river that Hampton was on the march. That officer sent word to de Salaberry and, in a flurry of orders and swift forced marching, de Salaberry gathered a mixed force at his Allan's Corners site. It included militia companies, two companies of Voltigeurs and one of Canadian Fencibles, and a party of twenty-two warriors of the Indian Department. While Hampton's main column emerged out of the deep woods and encamped at Spears's, de Salaberry's force feverishly began to prepare their defensive positions. In the rear, Stovin was casting about for whatever troops could be sent to support de Salaberry.

The spade-and-axe work of completing the positions, a series of breastworks thrown up on the banks of the ravines running to the woods at a right

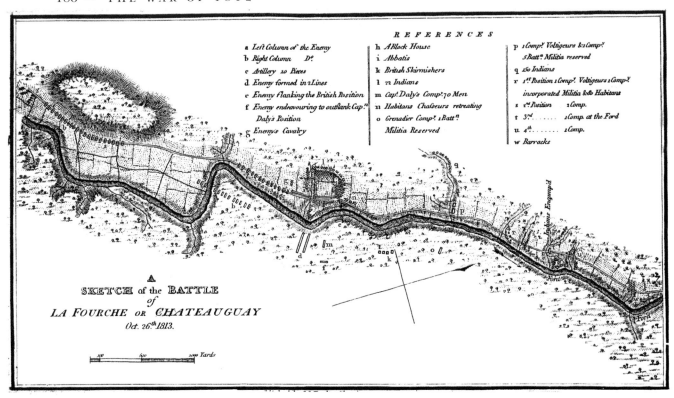

REFERENCES

a *Left Column of the Enemy*
b *Right Column   Do.*
c *Artillery 10 Pieces*
d *Enemy formed in 2 Lines*
e *Enemy flanking the British Position*
f *Enemy endeavouring to outflank Capt.*
   Daly's Position
g *Enemy's Cavalry*

h *A Block House*
i *Abbatis*
k *British Skirmishers*
l *Indians*
m *Capt. Daly's Compy. 70 Men*
n *Habitans Chasseurs retreating*
o *Grenadier Compy. 1 Batt.*
   Militia Reserved

p *1 Compy. Voltigeurs & 1 Compy.*
   5 Batt. Militia reserved
q *150 Indians*
r *1st Position 1 Compy. Voltigeurs 1 Compy.*
   incorporated Militia & Habitans
s *2d Position   2 Comp.*
t *3d. ...... 1 Comp. at the Ford*
u *4th. ...... 1 Comp.*
w *Barracks*

A
SKETCH of the BATTLE
of
LA FOURCHE OR CHATEAUGUAY
Oct. 26th 1813.

100   500   1000 Yards

angle to the river, gained added impetus from the sighting of mounted American patrols, almost as the Canadians arrived at the position. On October 24 de Salaberry made improvements to his position at Allan's Corners. Drawing working parties from the sedentary militia and providing them with a covering picket of Voltigeurs and Fencibles, he set about the construction of an "abatis," or log entanglement, in which trees are felled in the direction of the enemy and the branches sharpened into a hedge of spear-points. The ground before this position was then hurriedly cleared of cover as far as was practical. This new clearing adjoined the beginnings of more-or-less cleared land stretching back to Spears's, excluding the heavily wooded opposite bank of the river.

The mounted men de Salaberry had seen had not only scouted his position, but had also learned that a shallow ford existed just to the rear of the Canadian defences. This was reported to Hampton, and he determined to press forward with an attack, thinking "if it succeeded, we should be in possession of a position which we could hold as long as any doubts remained of what was passing above, and of the real part to be assigned to us." The

The overall plan of the battle on the banks of the Chateauguay, showing Hampton's main column, Purdy's flanking effort, and the series of prepared Canadian positions leading back to the ford at the rear. The Canadians were fortunate that Hampton was not as determined an adversary as he might have been.

A scene from the Galafilm/PTV Productions film War of 1812, *illustrating the bristling hedgehog defence of an abatis similar to that constructed by the Canadians at Chateauguay. Actors in the uniform of the Canadian Voltigeurs shelter behind the structure, awaiting action.*

ford offered a chance of outflanking the abatis and the series of fortified ravines, and Hampton had brought with him "guides," who were local men prepared to lead the Americans through any confusing woodland paths. These men now assured Hampton that they could lead an American party around de Salaberry's position to the ford in the rear.

Accordingly, at sunset on the evening of October 25, 1813, Hampton sent off a substantial flanking force, consisting of three of his regular regiments and some volunteers and light troops, under the command of Colonel Robert Purdy. This column crossed to the wooded eastern shore of the river and then set off on the overnight trek through the thick stands of white pine and cedar, which, their guides assured them, would put them at the ford in the rear of the Canadian position. There Purdy could storm across, while Hampton's main column attacked in front. As night fell, however, so did rain, and in the cold blackness the guides lost their way. In the grey, sodden light of dawn on Tuesday, October 26, Purdy was struggling through a cedar swamp still upriver of the abatis line, rather than approaching the ford; Hampton was falling in his main force on the muddy cart track at Spears's and preparing to advance; and de Salaberry was feverishly working on the abatis, aware of being poorly prepared for whatever attack was coming.

He had received reinforcements, however, and among the more remarkable efforts was a sixty-hour march to the advanced positions at Chateauguay by the First Light Battalion of the Lower Canada Select Embodied Militia, which was under the command of Lieutenant Colonel George Macdonnell of the Glengarry Light Infantry. After receiving orders on October 21 at Kingston to march immediately to de Salaberry's position, the battalion had gathered together flat-bottomed river scows and bateaux and made a perilous, storm-tossed descent of the St. Lawrence through the Long Sault, Coteau, Cedars, and Cascade rapids. After a brush with a severe storm at the western end of Lake St. Louis, they reached the village of Beauharnois on the evening of October 24. Setting off immediately at a quick pace along a narrow footpath that led towards de Salaberry, they arrived, drenched and exhausted, on the morning of October 25. After a discussion with de Salaberry, Macdonnell set the weary men to building a protective breastwork at the ford towards which Purdy would struggle that evening.

Under rainy, overcast skies on the morning of October 26, Hampton directed Izard to form his shivering, summer-clad infantry and accompanying dragoons on the cart track and, preceded by a small advance of light infantrymen, move on the abatis. As his troops trudged along the rutted cartway, Hampton awaited the expected sound of musketry from Purdy's rear attack. No such sound reassured him as he neared the stump-strewn ground before the dark line of de Salaberry's abatis, nor was there any evidence that Purdy had reached the ford.

Lieutenant Colonel George Macdonnell, known as "Red George" for his colouring, commanded the Canadian troops of the Glengarry Light Infantry, and had led the attack across the ice against Ogdensburg in February 1813. Before Chateauguay he led a select Light Battalion of Lower Canada militia on a trek from Kingston downriver and overland to de Salaberry's position. During the battle he commanded the reserve; he had bugles blown in the woods to deceive Hampton as to the actual size of the Canadian force.

The Canadian work parties were well into their morning labour when, at approximately 10:00 a.m., the first of the American light infantry was seen, deploying rapidly out into a line as they closed on the abatis. The protective screen of Voltigeurs and Fencibles exchanged a few shots with them before following the militia work parties in scrambling to cover behind the barrier. There they began to fire steadily at the American skirmish line, behind whom they could see the massed blue-and-white column waiting in the distance.

De Salaberry had been at one of the rear ravine positions when the firing broke out, and he galloped forward, ordering up with him the Light Company of the Fencibles, two companies of Voltigeurs, and the party of Indian Department warriors. They arrived, breathless after the fast trot through the wooded positions, to find the pickets and the sedentary militia banging away at the American skirmishers, but Hampton's column still unmoving in the distance. What de Salaberry did not know was that Hampton had received a note from Purdy, delivered by a man who had swum the river, telling Hampton that, as he feared, the flanking force had not yet reached the ford. Hampton now held back his main column, and this gave de Salaberry some time to deploy his little force to better effect.

As the firing at the abatis faded away, and a strange silence, broken only by an occasional shot, settled over the position, de Salaberry dispersed his companies. The warriors were sent off into the thick, swampy cedars beside the slash of the abatis, where their whoops and stealthy skill might deter any American flanking movement there. On the right, de Salaberry placed the red-coated Fencibles, with several sections of men out before the abatis again as skirmishers. In the centre, and on the angle formed by the abatis and the river, the two Voltigeur companies were posted, with the sedentary militia along the riverbank, where de Salaberry knew some kind of American flanking movement was being attempted.

Now posted, the Canadians looked to their priming and waited for a move from the halted mass of blue, white, and silver in the distance across the stump-dotted clearing. In the eerie silence, de Salaberry moved along the line as Tecumseh had done at Moraviantown, using first names, talking calmly and encouragingly, exuding confidence. He had sent a runner to Macdonnell, to warn him that something was being attempted on the wooded far shore, and on receipt of that message Macdonnell sent off

A rendering of the first moments of the battle, showing de Salaberry arriving at the abatis with additional troops, while Hampton's lead companies, under George Izard, deploy across the stump-dotted clearing. Elements of the uniforms are inaccurate, and the blockhouse was not built until after the battle.

two companies of his Light Battalion to the far shore beyond the ford that Purdy was attempting to reach, where a small picket of nervous local militia had been posted. Almost as they crossed, at about 11:00 a.m., two companies of Purdy's men burst out of the trees and stumbled on the militiamen, to the complete surprise of both. There was a startled exchange of point-blank volleys, and the American infantry fell back into the heavy bush, even as the militiamen fled, their blue tuques "flying in the wind." Macdonnell's men let the militiamen pass through them, and then closed with the confused Americans, whooping in warrior fashion. The exchange was brisk, as an eyewitness related: "There was quite a hot fire for a while, and several on both sides fell. I understood the Americans fell back because they did not anticipate resistance, and finding it, supposed the woods to be full of Indians." Purdy's two advance companies broke off their fight with the Canadians and pushed their way back through the wet cedar towards Purdy's main column, which was still struggling out of the swampy morass that had brought them no further downriver than the abatis line. Once again, an unexpected silence settled over the site.

In a colour sketch by modern French military artist Eugene Leliepvre, Canadian Voltigeurs are shown awaiting the call to action at Chateauguay, sheltering against the chill late October weather with blankets and a fire. With no formal encampment on the abatis line, the Canadians, though more warmly dressed than their American attackers, nonetheless suffered from exposure.

As noon passed, de Salaberry's men looked at the waiting American column and wondered what was happening within the depths of the trees on the far shore. Hampton sat waiting, even allowing fires to be lit beside the column, the men eating as they stood. Finally, Hampton had had enough. He sent off a message to Purdy, telling him to retire, cross the river, and rejoin the army, regardless of how far he had advanced. To Izard, he gave the order to advance. But then, at 2:00 p.m., a sudden storm of musketry burst from the far shore, and Hampton assumed this meant that Purdy had reached the ford after all. Izard was urged to assault the abatis line immediately.

The American column formed on the cart track and began to advance on the abatis. As it did so, a mounted American officer galloped forward to within shouting distance of the waiting Canadians and began to harangue them in poor French, calling on them to surrender. De Salaberry seized a musket from one of the Voltigeurs and fired at the officer, dropping him from his horse in mid-sentence, then cried out the command to open fire. A roar of musketry burst from the abatis, and at this Izard wheeled his huge column into line facing the abatis and also opened fire. The thunderous volleys sent the Fencibles skirmishers sprinting for the abatis, and a shout went up along the American line.

De Salaberry sensed a moment of crisis, and ordered his men to cheer in response. The hidden warriors on the swampy right now raised their whooping cries, and de Salaberry ordered his buglers to sound the "advance." Macdonnell, who was now at the first reserve line, then "caused the bugles to be sounded in all directions, so as to induce the enemy to believe that we were in far greater numbers." This din confused Hampton as to the actual strength of the force facing him and he paused; the moment when his massive American line might have surged over the abatis and its several hundred defenders was averted by a clever ruse.

The fire of Izard's men now slackened, as if their attention was directed to the other side of the river. De Salaberry was finally able to glimpse Purdy's men almost abreast the abatis line and, downstream, the red-coated Embodied Militia companies closing the gap on them. As he recalled later, de Salaberry spotted the senior officer of the Canadians, a bilingual Irishman named Charles Daly, and leaped up on a stump to call out instructions to him, "cautioning him to answer in the same language

[French] that they might not be understood by the enemy." Within a few minutes the two Canadian companies closed the gap with Purdy's men, and there was a new crescendo of musketry, the thick smoke lying low amid the trees. The fight broke into confused hand-to-hand action, the Canadians going down under waves of American infantrymen, as Purdy's numbers began to tell. Intent on surrounding and finishing off the two Canadian companies, Purdy's men burst out of the woods onto the riverbank, only to be astonished as they looked across almost directly at the main Canadian position, where de Salaberry, still atop his stump ("grimpé sur une souche," as he said later), was eyeing them coolly through

A company of United States Army infantry in the dress of the 1813 campaign, deployed into line as they might have been at Chateauguay or Crysler's Farm. The front rank have knelt and are "presenting" their muskets, ready for the order to fire. The rear rank are at the "ready" position, having cocked their weapons, and are now waiting to present and fire after the front rank has done so. A trained infantryman could fire and reload his smoothbore flintlock musket every twenty seconds, faster than the militiamen shown on the flanks of the company, who are reloading their weapons less assuredly.

a telescope above the waiting levelled muzzles of the sedentary militiamen. At a bark from de Salaberry the line of muskets opened a murderous fire across the narrow river.

The torrent of enfilading musketry cut down Purdy's men as they struggled to regain the forest cover, leaving bodies littering the river's edge. Purdy broke off any further attempt at advance and began to retire downstream. A messenger swam again to Hampton, but Hampton's mind was already made up on the basis of what he himself could see of the disaster across the river. He ordered a surprised Izard – whose line was still virtually intact – to withdraw, re-form on the roadway, and march back to the encampment. As de Salaberry's men stared in some disbelief, Izard's men faced about, re-formed in column on the roadway in good order, and marched off. The Canadians held their fire and watched them go in silence, the sound of the fifes and drums diminishing in the distance.

Now the shadowy figures of the warriors moved after them in pursuit, and de Salaberry sent out men to recover the American wounded. They were carried to a stone farmhouse a short distance behind the battle line, and the Canadians returned to the abatis, waiting in the rain for Hampton to return. But for de Salaberry's men, the battle was over. They slept at the abatis and at the reserve lines, huddled in the miserable rain, listening to distant musketry as Purdy's column spent a hellish night in the cedar swamp. The next morning, Purdy managed to build a floating log bridge and get his men across it to the cart track, the warriors picking men off with long shots as they stumbled along the slippery logs.

By the second nightfall Hampton's army was back in its encampment, having left some seventy dead, a number of wounded, and sixteen prisoners behind. The cart trail was strewn with discarded equipment, drums, provisions, muskets, and other gear from Purdy's retreating men. De Salaberry had lost only a few men, mostly in the sharp fighting against Purdy.

A rendering of American Light Infantry men in action, using the two-man firing unit that allowed one man to protect the other during the lengthy loading process. The majority of the Canadian troops at Chateauguay were trained in these tactics, in contrast with the formations of Hampton's troops, who delivered mass volleys by companies.

As they might have appeared in Hampton's formation at the battle on the Chateauguay River, American officers observe the action while a dragoon messenger waits to be sent off with orders. While infantrymen of the era normally marched everywhere, officers above the rank of a company officer were usually mounted on horseback.

At his muddy encampment, Hampton called a council of war, asking his officers a leading question:

> Is it advisable, under existing circumstances, to renew the attack on the enemy's position; and, if not, what position is it advisable for the army to take, until it can receive advice of the advance of the grand army down the Saint Lawrence?

He was no doubt pleased with the reply:

> It is the unanimous opinion of this council that it is necessary, for the preservation of this army and the fulfillment of the ostensible views of the government, that we immediately return by orderly marches to such a position [Chateauguay Four Corners] as will secure our communications with the United States, either to retire into winter quarters or be ready to strike below.

A rear view of an American line of "skirmishers," which were light-infantry troops sent ahead of the main battle line of an army to engage the enemy. The Glengarry Light Infantry and Canadian Voltigeurs were Canadian regiments trained during the War of 1812 to fight in this manner.

At noon of October 28, the return march to New York state began, the column harassed by the Caughnawagas who had fought so well, and for little credit, at Beaver Dams. The warriors gave the jittery American infantrymen little peace in their last encampment on Canadian soil, attacking them on the night of October 29 to kill one sentry and wound seven. By the next day, de Salaberry received word that Hampton was back at Four Corners and the immediate threat had passed.

Prevost had arrived at de Salaberry's position, and was full of praise for the steadfastness of the Canadian troops. De Salaberry later remarked, "I hope he is satisfied, though he appeared cold." It would take several weeks for the disproportionate impact of this extended skirmish victory – and what de Salaberry and Macdonnell had achieved – to be known. The news would reach Wilkinson, but only a week later. Hampton waited until November 8 to send off word on what had transpired, and the news landed in the midst of a troubled progress of Wilkinson's "grand army," a progress that had just suffered a reverse of its own.

At the beginning of October, it might have seemed that the only threat to the potential final conquest of heartland Canada was the coming of cold weather; soon, however, it became clear that Hampton's hated partner, Wilkinson, was a threat to success as well. Wilkinson was enormously reluctant to risk anything that might lead to failure, and he was ill again, his southern constitution suffering in the rigours of the northern fall. His force was enormous, consisting of 8,000 infantry, 38 field guns, 20 larger seige guns, two regiments of cavalry, and a mountain of supplies and equipment. Armstrong had ordered some 300 row barges and boats built to transport the army towards Montreal, and the secretary of war had paced the windy waterfront of Sackets Harbor, crowded with the boats and Chauncey's squadron, and fidgeted over Wilkinson's inertia.

Finally, having waited past the clear, golden days of September into a cold and stormy October that bedevilled Hampton, Wilkinson got the huge force away from Sackets on October 17, only to be struck by a horrendous storm as the warm weather ended. He was stranded on Grenadier Island, four miles from the mouth of the St. Lawrence, suffering through ten inches of unseasonal snow. Damaged boats were abandoned, and the troops put off again. Chauncey patrolled Kingston harbour – where Yeo stayed at anchor and refused to come out – and sent off some of his vessels with Wilkinson's labouring open boats, to ferry horses, guns, and supplies as far as Ogdensburg, New York. The descent of the river went smoothly at first, although the troops suffered horribly from the cold and rain.

Behind Wilkinson, Prevost, if at first taken in by the threat of an attack against Kingston, had pulled much of the garrison back to the Montreal area, including Macdonnell's forces, and their boats were on the river just ahead of Wilkinson's. The Kingston garrison commander also sent off a force after Wilkinson, knowing that practically every American infantryman east of Detroit was in Wilkinson's boats. Under Lieutenant Colonel Joseph Morrison, some six hundred men of the British 49th and 89th regiments clambered into boats of their own and set off in pursuit, while Yeo sent along a clutch of small protecting gunboats under the command of William Howe Mulcaster, who had captained *Royal George* on Lake Ontario. Morrison stopped at Fort Wellington (present-day Prescott), across the river from Ogdensburg, to collect some light troops. There he was joined by some of de Salaberry's Voltigeurs, the Canadian Fencibles, a clutch of warriors, and

Prescott, viewed from Ogdensburg harbour. The towns of Prescott, in Canada, and Ogdensburg, in the United States, could not avoid the war due to their location on the strategic St. Lawrence River. The people of both towns nonetheless maintained friendships and trade, and assisted one another in spite of the conflict.

a militia gun crew with a single six-pounder gun. It was a little enough force to pursue and challenge a horde of eight thousand men.

Wilkinson had already decided to ignore Fort Wellington, choosing to disembark his troops out of the fort's gun range and march them through Ogdensburg to re-embark below the town. The flotilla of open boats was run past the fort during the night and, with the outward appearance of efficiency, all were re-embarked and the descent continued. By November 8, Wilkinson had halted the armada at a point eighteen miles below Ogdensburg, having traversed half the distance to Montreal, but having reached the beginning of the treacherous series of rapids that stretched all the way down the river to Lake St. Louis, outside the city itself. He knew Morrison was pursuing him, but knew as well that Morrison's force was too small to defeat him; Hampton's letter with its dismaying news was still two days away from arriving. Wilkinson's antennae for danger were nonetheless quivering, and, if he was competent in very little else, he had a keen sense of a risky situation. Predictably, he called a council of war, and asked his officers if the expedition should be abandoned. A majority replied that the expedition was in great danger, but should proceed, as "we know of no alternative."

Ahead of Wilkinson lay the Long Sault Rapids, almost six miles in length. The huge armada would be at its most defenceless going through them, and the Canadian north shore needed to be secured to prevent any ambush. To accomplish this task, Wilkinson landed a substantial force under Alexander Macomb – the leading unit headed by the redoubtable Winfield Scott – which was ordered to march downriver and secure the bank as far as Cornwall. A second force to back up Macomb was put ashore under General Jacob Brown, and it set off for Cornwall as well. To protect the rear, and the progress of the boats down through the treacherous rapids, Wilkinson set ashore a brigade under Brigadier General John Boyd.

To run the rapids during the day, the boats had to go through in batches, and the waiting craft anchored in groups just below Crysler Island in the river. Soon, Wilkinson received word from Macomb and Brown that their troops had done their duty; a British and Canadian attack at Hoople's Creek had been brushed aside, and the road to Cornwall was now clear. But Macomb's and Brown's troops were exhausted, wet and chilled in the continuing rain, and had brought no tents. Wilkinson instructed the boats to keep on once they had run the Long Sault Rapids and carry supplies to Macomb, with orders to Boyd to follow the last group of boats through and remain watchful for Morrison's pursuit. It was at this moment that Wilkinson, lying ill in his camp bed, received the news that Morrison's force was in sight upriver. It was the morning of November 11, 1813.

Morrison came on in column along the muddy shore road, while, in the river, Mulcaster brought his gunboats ahead and began to loft rounds at the American boats waiting above the rapids. As Morrison saw Boyd's brigade retiring downriver, he deployed out into line, as if to tempt the Americans to turn and fight. Morrison had entered open fields belonging to John Crysler,

Jacob "Smuggler" Brown, who commanded a portion of Wilkinson's force descending the St. Lawrence and would later command American forces on the Niagara frontier in the fruitless fighting of 1814.

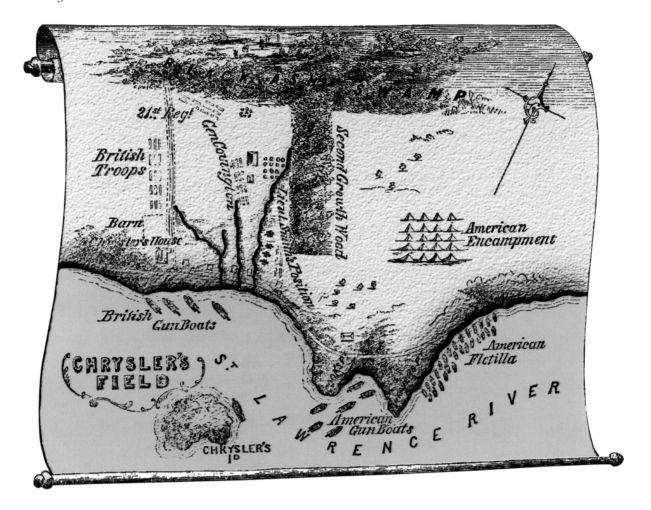

and his deployment of his column was similar to that of de Salaberry at Chateauguay – or of Procter at Moraviantown, for that matter – although Morrison kept his formations tightly "dressed," or aligned with one another. Close to the river, where Mulcaster's gunboats provided some cover, he placed the few militiamen and his gun. In the centre of the line, he placed his two regular regiments, Brock's old 49th and the Irishmen of the 89th, with the 49th closest to the river. On their left flank, where the wooded terrain began, he sent the warriors and the Voltigeurs, and then screened the whole force with a line of warriors, Fencibles, and Voltigeurs in light infantry formation. It was a cold, wet day, the ground sodden from heavy rain during the night and, as Morrison's main battle line stood patiently, the light-infantry screen moved forward and began to fire at Boyd's men. Boyd was in a difficult situation: the boats were proceeding through the

The disposition of the British and American troops at Crysler's Farm, where Lieutenant Colonel Morrison's pursuing force from Kingston was attacked by Wilkinson's rearguard as the Americans tried to ferry their main body of troops through the rapids.

Long Sault Rapids; Brown's and Macomb's men were drawing down-river; the link to the supply of ammunition was stretching longer with every minute. Boyd determined to send two brigades back to dispose of Morrison's force, with some artillery support and some cavalry, and to carry on with the rest of his force downriver.

Robert Swartout's brigade of infantry was the first to turn, slog back through the mud, and engage Morrison. The Canadian skirmish line retired in good order, but, when Swartout moved to outflank Morrison by penetrating the woods on Morrison's left flank, he ran into a fierce fight with the warriors and the Voltigeurs. As this raged, the 89th Regiment faced to their left and began to deliver crack, thunderclap volleys that halt-ed Swartout's men. They pulled back, re-formed into a line of their own, and a test of will and discipline began. In support of Swartout, the second American brigade arrived and deployed rapidly into line, under the command of General Leonard Covington, along with an American gun battery. This battery opened fire on the tightly arrayed formation of British regulars, and gaps began to open in their line. The British held their ground, how-ever, and a musketry battle ensued, with the large-but-unwieldy American force unable either to shake the discipline of Morrison's bloodied, deter-mined centre, or to outflank the warriors and the Voltigeurs.

The crisis of the battle came when Morrison sensed exhaustion in the Americans and ordered an advance. The bayonets came down, and the 89th Regiment closed on the American gun that had hurt them so much. Though halted briefly by American cavalry, the 89th fought them off and took the gun. Unable to achieve victory against Morrison's steady line, his troops drooping with fatigue and separated yet farther from their supplies, Boyd gave up the field to Morrison. The affair was a bloody one, with Morrison losing a fifth of his men, and the Americans almost five hundred, including General Covington. It did not stop Wilkinson; but, in concert with the letter Wilkinson was about to receive, it won the battle over Wilkinson's spirit.

Wilkinson had written to Hampton on November 6, directing him to meet Wilkinson's army at Saint Regis on the St. Lawrence, just upriver from Montreal; the letter he received on November 12, in which Hampton finally informed him of his having turned back, coming as it did the day after his rearguard had been defeated by Morrison, gave the ailing general the

opportunity he had been seeking. He called a council of war, which advised him that, with Hampton's retirement, the plan of the campaign had been ruined. Wilkinson wrote to Hampton in language that landed the blame right where Wilkinson hoped it would land – and gave him the excuse to end the campaign against Montreal.

> Headquarters, near Cornwall (U.C.)
> November 12th, 1813

Sir

I had this day the honour to receive your letter of the 8th instant, by Colonel Atkinson, and want language to express my sorrow for your determination not to join the division under your command, with the troops under my immediate orders.

As such resolution defeats the grand objects of the campaign in this quarter, which, before the receipt of your letter, were thought to be completely within our power, no suspicion being entertained that you would decline the junction directed, it will oblige us to take post at French Mills, on Salmon River, or in their vicinity, for the winter.

I have the honour to be, Etc.
Jas. Wilkinson

Adam Scott's panoramic depiction of the Battle of Crysler's Farm shows, in the upper right, the steady British line of the 49th and 89th regiments confronting the piecemeal attacks of Wilkinson's rearguard. In the foreground, behind the American battle line, American troops who had attempted to outflank the British position are retiring, while behind them, the almost continuous firing of the American line is answered by carefully controlled company and platoon volleys from the British, evinced by the regularly spaced smoke of their firing. The view is south, and behind the struggle lies the St. Lawrence River.

The most serious invasion threat Canada had faced in the war had passed, due in large part to the steady defence of their small position by the Canadian regulars, militia, and warriors of de Salaberry and Macdonnell at Chateauguay, and the unyielding courage of Morrison's men against Boyd at Crysler's Farm.

Wilkinson took his army off to miserable quarters in huts at French Mills (now Fort Covington, New York), on the Salmon River, lining the riverbank with his now-useless boats. Secretary of War Armstrong, who had returned to the warmth of Washington after seeing Wilkinson off from Sackets Harbor, digested the failure of the expedition, and overrode Wilkinson's orders. The general was told instead to pack up camp in January when the roads were frozen solid, send Jacob Brown off with two thousand men to Sackets Harbor, and march with the rest to Plattsburg, where Hampton had retired.

By February Wilkinson was ready, and he set fire to the rows of huts, the three hundred boats, the defensive blockhouses he had built – the fire could be seen for miles, far off on the Canadian shore of the St. Lawrence – and, after sending Brown's column to Sackets Harbor, Wilkinson began the long march to Plattsburg, the men trudging through the cold with their supplies hauled on sledges. Even in this forlorn journey, Wilkinson was not spared humiliation. A force of some eleven hundred British, Canadians, and warriors struck south from Coteau du Lac on the St. Lawrence. Moving quickly on snowshoes and fighting the irregular forest warfare at which the warriors and Lower Canadians were so proficient, they were directed by Colonel Hercules Scott in a sweep that took them from a brush with Wilkinson's rearguard near French Mills to communities along Wilkinson's route of march. They pursued him almost to Plattsburg, capturing nearly a hundred sledges laden with baggage and provisions. Scott's force returned to Canada unmolested.

It had been the final nail in the coffin of a campaign that had thrown away for the United States the moment of complete victory, a victory that Harrison's and Perry's victories in the west, and the bottling up of the British in Burlington, had seemed to guarantee. In the west, the British had been driven from the Detroit frontier and Lake Erie, and Indian power had been smashed with the defeat of Tecumseh. But in the east, the tenacious defences at Chateauguay and Crysler's Farm had denied the United States total success. In many American minds, there was little left to justify a continuation of the war. But now a darker element entered the contest: thoughts turned not to strategic gain, but to exacting revenge on the enemy. The last major drama of 1813 on Canadian soil did much to paint the war's canvas in these new and bloodier colours.

In Fort George, in the occupied village of Newark on the Niagara frontier, George McClure still held sway over the countryside of the Niagara Peninsula. The violence and plundering of his New York militia and of the Canadian turncoats was unchecked except by the underground resistance of Canadian settlers, who ambushed raiding parties and fought savage encounters with them in farmyards and country lanes, where little quarter was asked or given. Vincent, bottled up at Burlington with his troops and the remains of Procter's force, could not prevent these horrors. But then in November came the message to McClure that the grand campaign against

Montreal had failed, and that the tenuous British route of supply to Burlington would not be cut. McClure had obtained from Secretary of War Armstrong himself a written document authorizing him to destroy Newark if "military necessity" dictated.

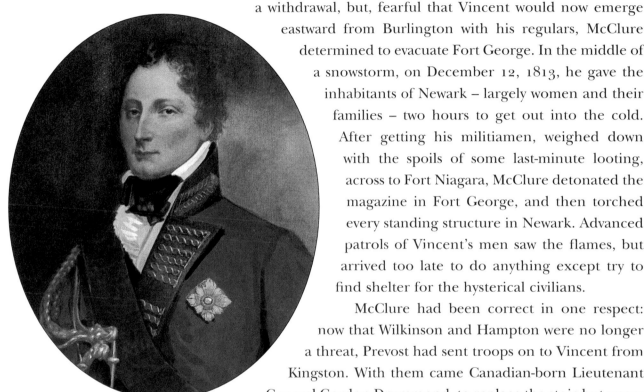

He took some time after the news of Wilkinson's debacle to organize a withdrawal, but, fearful that Vincent would now emerge eastward from Burlington with his regulars, McClure determined to evacuate Fort George. In the middle of a snowstorm, on December 12, 1813, he gave the inhabitants of Newark – largely women and their families – two hours to get out into the cold. After getting his militiamen, weighed down with the spoils of some last-minute looting, across to Fort Niagara, McClure detonated the magazine in Fort George, and then torched every standing structure in Newark. Advanced patrols of Vincent's men saw the flames, but arrived too late to do anything except try to find shelter for the hysterical civilians.

McClure had been correct in one respect: now that Wilkinson and Hampton were no longer a threat, Prevost had sent troops on to Vincent from Kingston. With them came Canadian-born Lieutenant General Gordon Drummond, to replace the stoic-but-weary Vincent, and Major General Phineas Riall. When the relief column of British and Canadians arrived at the blackened ruins and learned the extent of the mistreatment the Canadian inhabitants had suffered at the hands of McClure's men, a black and bitter mood of revenge set in, beginning with Drummond. Six days after McClure's evacuation of Fort George, Drummond mounted a savage punitive raid under Colonel John Murray against Fort Niagara.

Just over five hundred men crossed the river at night, equipped with scaling ladders and axes, and under orders not to fire, but only to use the cold steel of the bayonet. The first men ashore killed the American sentries outside the gate in

Gordon Drummond was a Canadian career soldier who, in late 1813, took command on the Niagara frontier, and was determined, like Brock, to carry the war to the enemy. He would command the British and Canadian line in the bloody stalemate at Lundy's Lane in 1814, and fail in an attempt to take Fort Erie, which was later abandoned and blown up by the Americans. Following the War of 1812 he would serve briefly as Governor General of the Canadas.

silence, found that the gate was unbarred, and threw it open. Murray's men came in at the run, still maintaining their rigid silence. The duty company of Americans emerged from the guardhouse and managed to get off a sputtering volley before the white-lipped British and Canadians were on them, bayonetting them to a man. In the soldiers' quarters some firing went on for several minutes until the British killed them as well. Some eighty men died under the British and Canadian bayonets until a plea to accept surrender broke the killing rage, and more than three hundred men were taken. Only twenty managed to escape, to warn McClure at Buffalo.

There was more to Drummond's plan. At the distant boom of a Fort Niagara gun, fired as a signal by Murray, Phineas Riall upriver sent five hundred warriors across the river against the little village of Lewiston, New York, with five hundred redcoats at their heels. Drummond's orders had been clear: no repetition of McClure's wanton cruelty or burning of homes. But Riall disregarded the orders, and, after a feeble militia resistance was swept away, he allowed the burning of every home along a twenty-five-mile swath from Fort Niagara itself to Tonawanda Creek. It was as heinous an act as McClure's had been, and signalled the darker horror surfacing in a war that had begun with niceties and the exchange of courtesies.

Fort Niagara, viewed from Newark (Niagara-on-the-Lake). Fort Niagara was the scene of a ruthless bayonet attack by British and Canadian troops enraged at McClure's burning of the village of Newark. Following its capture, virtually the entire American Niagara frontier was put to the torch.

Continuing the retaliatory destruction along the Niagara frontier, Phineas Riall's British troops attack and destroy Buffalo, New York, on Lake Erie just above the mouth of the Niagara River, in the winter of 1813.

Riall acted in the same manner some days later, when, on December 29, he crossed with fifteen hundred men near Fort Erie and attacked the village of Black Rock. After dispersing another weak militia resistance, Riall burned ships he found in the ice in the harbour, and then pressed on to the village of Buffalo, New York. There the torch was used again, and, by the time Riall took his troops back across the Niagara River, the entire Niagara frontier of New York, from Fort Niagara to Buffalo, was a blackened ruin. It was not a proud moment.

The war had now become a theatre for the worst instincts of men, and there was a year of it ahead, with no clear reason, after 1813's exhausting struggle, why such destruction and brutality should continue between societies that a foreign visitor would find almost indistinguishable in speech, manner, and ideals. But the burden of pain and suffering was about to increase.

CHAPTER FOUR

"The rockets' red glare"

THE BLOODY CONCLUSION AND CANADA'S SURVIVAL

DURING THE HARSH WINTER THAT settled in over the Canadas after the 1813 campaign, there was a sense of exhaustion, but also a sense of a catastrophe barely averted. Everything west of Lake Ontario, except for the northern reaches of the Great Lakes, lay at Washington's mercy. But the defences of the

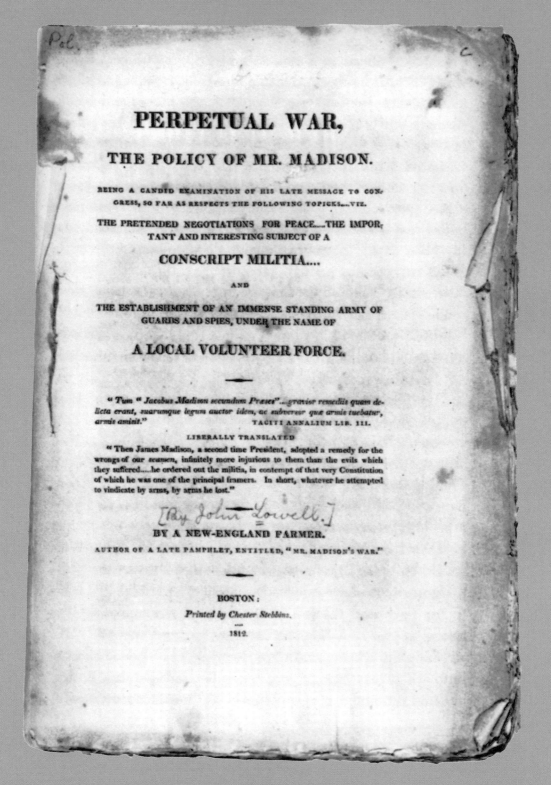

PERPETUAL WAR,

THE POLICY OF MR. MADISON.

BEING A CANDID EXAMINATION OF HIS LATE MESSAGE TO CON-
GRESS, SO FAR AS RESPECTS THE FOLLOWING TOPICKS....VIZ.

THE PRETENDED NEGOTIATIONS FOR PEACE.....THE IMPOR-
TANT AND INTERESTING SUBJECT OF A

CONSCRIPT MILITIA....

AND

THE ESTABLISHMENT OF AN IMMENSE STANDING ARMY OF
GUARDS AND SPIES, UNDER THE NAME OF

A LOCAL VOLUNTEER FORCE.

———

" Tum " Jacobus Madison secundum Præses"....gravior remediis quam de-
licta erant, suarumque legum auctor idem, ac subversor quæ armis tuebatur,
armis amisit."
TACITI ANNALIUM LIB. III.

LIBERALLY TRANSLATED

" Then James Madison, a second time President, adopted a remedy for the
wrongs of our seamen, infinitely more injurious to them than the evils which
they suffered....he ordered out the militia, in contempt of that very Constitution
of which he was one of the principal framers. In short, whatever he attempted
to vindicate by arms, by arms he lost."

[By John Lowell.]

BY A NEW-ENGLAND FARMER.

AUTHOR OF A LATE PAMPHLET, ENTITLED, " MR. MADISON'S WAR."

———

BOSTON :
Printed by Chester Stebbins.
———
1812.

Perpetual War *was one of a number of anonymous publications – this one, authored by a "New England Farmer," was in fact written by John Lowell – that appeared in New England, opposing the war with Canada. Unhappiness with the war in New England was so intense that an active secessionist movement arose, determined to sever New England from the United States if the ruinous war continued.*

heartland had held, if just, and a good wheat harvest and the energy of middlemen in Vermont and New York – who kept Canada well supplied with American beef – meant that survival and endurance might still be possible. The American plan for overall conquest, in both 1812 and 1813, had failed except in the remote west.

And now from Europe came word of Napoleon's defeat at Leipzig, and of the heartening possibility that Great Britain's enormous war machine might increasingly be available to deal with what London had seen as a costly but remote Canadian sideshow. The British administration of Lord Robert Castlereagh had heard of the consternation in Washington over the repeated military failures; of President James Madison's own secret distaste for the war; of the growing anger against it in New England, where serious minds were considering the possibilities of secession from the union, or even a bizarre conjunction with the Canadas, New Brunswick, and Nova Scotia. Perhaps Washington would listen to a peace overture. On November 4, a letter from Castlereagh to Madison proposing peace talks began to make its slow passage by frigate towards Washington.

John Quincy Adams was serving as American ambassador to Russia when he was selected by President Madison to chair the commission that would discuss peace terms with the British government. Reserved and fair-minded, he obtained remarkably good terms for the United States in the treaty signed in December 1814, and would later serve as secretary of state, and finally as president of the United States.

By January, Madison had accepted the offer of talks – though the war would continue – and had selected a team of negotiators that ranged from the War Hawk Henry Clay, the adamant enemy of an Indian "homeland" triumphant over Tecumseh's death, to Treasury Secretary Albert Gallatin, who warned Madison of impending national bankruptcy if the war continued. Chairing the team was John Quincy Adams, whose astute reserve was meant to balance any extremism. The talks were to take place in

Ghent, Belgium, and Adams and the others made their way there to await the British delegation.

Smarting from the overall failure of the 1813 campaign, Secretary of War Armstrong was approaching 1814 with new determination, part of which saw him replace the inept and lacklustre Revolutionary War veterans and put the American army on the Canadian frontier in the control of capable men. The Detroit frontier was already secured, and he left it in the hands of militia; Lake Erie was in any event an American lake. On the Niagara frontier he promoted the able Winfield Scott to command, and on Lake Champlain he set aside Wade Hampton in favour of George Izard, who had behaved with cool competence during the Chateauguay affair. For Hampton's rival, James Wilkinson, who had tried and failed at one more fruitless invasion attempt, the war was over as well by spring. Armstrong put Jacob Brown, who had led the shore force down the St. Lawrence in 1813, in overall command of the campaign against the Canadas. Armstrong determined that Montreal, again, would be the ultimate target, with Kingston to serve as a preliminary objective. And if Sir James Lucas Yeo's squadron at Kingston was intact and undefeated, so was Isaac Chauncey's squadron at Sackets Harbor. In support of Izard at Plattsburg, there was Macdonough's vastly improved squadron, which kept Pring safely away at Ile aux Noix, on the Richelieu. The military portents for success were there, with capable officers now in place, naval support on the lakes available, and a general thirst in the American military mind for a success that would bring vindication. But the unanswered question was whether that could be achieved before the men who had beaten Napoleon began arriving in Canada.

The American military's renewed determination was not shared by the nation at large. The increasing activities of the Royal Navy had destroyed American international trade and brought coastal shipping to a standstill. Internal trade in the United States was forced to move by road, and inflation was uncontrollable. Deprived of any consistent income source, the United States government faced bankruptcy – and the real political threat of the secessionist movement in New England. In addition, even the general public realized that Napoleon's defeat meant the British were turning their attention and military resources to resolving the irritant of "Brother Jonathan's" war. The British very clearly intended to support the Canadian garrisons sufficiently to prevent their defeat, but were also intending to use their greatest strength – sea power – in their argument with the United States. Given the enormous and virtually undefended Atlantic seaboard, the potential destructiveness of that power was all too apparent. Goaded on by the War Hawks, resented by New England, warned by his officials of coming national bankruptcy, Madison stumbled on with the war, quietly hoping for a settlement that would allow escape from the mess without grievous loss.

For Sir George Prevost at Quebec, the impending collapse of Napoleon and the increasing interest being displayed by Whitehall in his lonely struggle were sources of hope, if not immediate relief. The Lower Canadian defences were sound, and had proven capable, if fortunate. In Upper Canada, all was more or less abandoned west of Lake Ontario, but Drummond held the Niagara frontier, with the forces at Burlington to support him. The long Lake Erie shore was his vulnerable spot and, if outflanked there or defeated on the frontier, he could retire as Vincent had done in 1813. York was still Prevost's, and the vital citadel of Kingston,

"A Sketch for the Regent's Speech on Mad-ass-son's Insanity." A British cartoon of 1812 asserting that Madison's declaration of war against Great Britain would not go unpunished. Symbolically, Britannia is shown handing the shield of her protection to an American Indian.

A SCENE ON LAKE ONTARIO

Isaac Chauncey's flagship, the General Pike *(left), is shown manoeuvring to engage Sir James Yeo's flagship,* Wolfe *(right). Through caution or circumstance, the rival fleets on Lake Ontario never came to a climactic battle with one another.*

where the Royal Navy Lake Ontario Squadron was still intact. If Yeo had not won control of Lake Ontario, he had not lost it either, and the potential was still there for a sudden, decisive victory over Chauncey – as there was for a catastrophic loss. Britain was relatively secure on the upper lakes, where the British were maintaining their supply route to the western Indians, trekking up overland from York to Lake Simcoe and on to Georgian Bay, then on by schooner to the British post at Mackinac.

Meanwhile, for the western part of Upper Canada, the year 1814 would bring home the final reality of what war meant beyond the parades of uniformed men and the waving of flags. Raiding parties swept up the Thames River – where a small British force sent to try and stop them was defeated at Longwood on March 5 – or stormed ashore from boats anywhere along the Lake Erie shoreline. It was a dirty, bitter process of looting and burning, which did not spare even those settlers who had once welcomed the Americans. Again, as on the Niagara frontier, renegade Canadians rode with the American gangs, using the opportunity to settle old scores with all the pitiless vengefulness of men engaged in civil war. After a summer of such depredations, the valley of the Thames River and the shoreline of Lake Erie from Amherstburg to the mouth of the Grand River and eastward would be a torched wasteland of ruined farms and mills, and the population

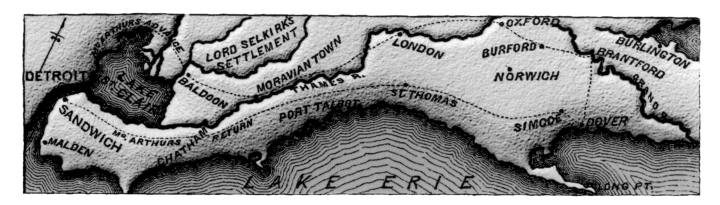

This map shows the route of Duncan McArthur's raid of 1814 into southern Upper Canada with mounted American militia. Harrison's victory on the Thames led the British to abandon any real attempt to defend territory west of Lake Ontario, and Canadian settlements along the Lake Erie shore particularly suffered at the hands of "marauders."

would suffer under the continuing lash, waiting for it to end – somehow.

The most dramatic, and almost the last, of these punishing raids would be carried out by a force of eight hundred mounted American irregulars under Duncan McArthur, who would spend three weeks in the fall of 1814 pillaging from the mouth of the Thames eastward to within a few hours' ride of Burlington, largely pushing aside the few units Drummond could send against him. McArthur's force returned to the Detroit frontier intact, having added another layer to the legacy of bitterness for the Upper Canadians.

In the Old Northwest, the year began with the news, in the spring of 1814, that the Americans had taken Prairie du Chien, a western British post north of the present city of Dubuque, Iowa, and were planning to retake Mackinac, Colonel Robert McDouall and a party of seamen and infantry made a remarkable trek from the mouth of the Nottawasaga River to Mackinac. When no American attack on Mackinac materialized, McDouall put together a force of warriors and Michigan Fencibles – largely fur-trade men – and sent them off on June 28 under William McKay to make another epic trek by canoe and open boat to Prairie du Chien, astonishing the Americans by retaking it. McDouall, however, had to do without McKay's men when he was presented with the arrival at Mackinac of the American force meant to recapture it. The American Lake Erie squadron, including the U.S. brig *Niagara*, arrived on August 4 bearing 750 infantry under the command of Colonel George Groghan, who had repulsed Henry Procter at Fort Stephenson.

Groghan landed his force and advanced on the fort, only to be ambushed by McDouall, who had less than half his strength. Once again, after a sharp little battle McDouall could easily have lost, the presence of the warriors induced Groghan to give up the attempt and retire to his boats. The American naval commander left two schooners, *Scorpion* and *Tigress*, hovering about the Straits of Mackinac to prevent Fort Mackinac being resupplied, and sailed south.

As they swung into Georgian Bay, they found the British supply schooner *Nancy* at sheltered anchor a short distance up the Nottawasaga River. When they sailed off, *Nancy* was a burning wreck, and Royal Navy Lieutenant Miller Worsley stood on the beach watching her burn and vowing revenge. He, with a party of seamen and Royal Newfoundland Regiment men, made a courageous canoe-and-open-boat trek to Mackinac. On arrival there he was able to obtain that revenge when, working with Lieutenant Andrew Bulger of the Newfoundland men, he used four boats, followed by Indian canoes, to pounce on and capture *Tigress*, and then used her to capture *Scorpion*. It was a moment of some vindication for Worsley – and for British and Canadian fortunes in the western waters after so much defeat and loss.

The Nancy *(above) was a British supply schooner on the Upper Lakes that was burned by an American force when they found her hidden in the mouth of the Nottawasaga River. The Americans were returning from a failed bid to retake Fort Mackinac. The* Nancy*'s crew avenged her by capturing two American schooners in daring boat attacks.*

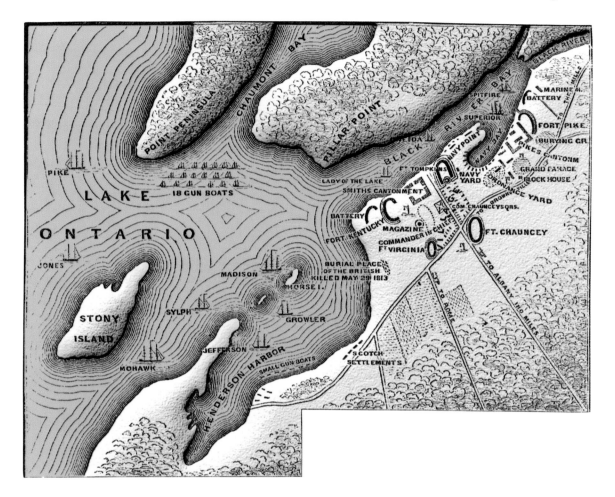

A detailed plan of the American naval base at Sackets Harbor in 1814, showing Chauncey's squadron dispersed in a defensive anchorage pattern. Sackets Harbor had been unsuccessfully attacked by the British in May, 1813, and was the base from which Wilkinson's huge army had set out for the descent on Montreal.

On lakes Ontario and Erie and on the Niagara frontier, 1814 was also to be a pivotal year. The promotion of Jacob Brown to Major General with the responsibility for prosecution of the northern war brought him to Sackets Harbor in the spring of 1814, where Chauncey's fleet was intact, and Secretary of War Armstrong was clearly intending to repeat the attempt on Montreal. Brown – known as "Smuggler" Brown by his troops – was a capable officer, who displayed neither hesitation nor indolence. But at Sackets Harbor he faced the changed attitude of Commodore Isaac Chauncey, who had been relatively successful against Yeo, but who had now gone from being an aggressive officer to a cautious man obsessed with the fear of losing his fleet in an action with Yeo, or in an attack on Kingston. As Yeo found himself in virtually the same psychological state, both men had resorted to a shipbuilders' war over the winter, and Yeo was temporarily ahead, having now eight ships of war, and having launched the *Princess Charlotte*, 44 guns, and the *Prince Regent*, 60 guns, as soon as the receding ice permitted. Brown therefore arrived to find Chauncey in no frame of mind to consider risking an attack on Kingston with his temporarily inferior squadron and Brown's two thousand infantry. In a remarkable case of misconstrued orders, Chauncey was to be spared the confrontation he wished to avoid.

In March of 1814, Armstrong wrote to Brown with clear and explicit orders:

> You will immediately consult with Commodore Chauncey about the readiness of the fleet for a descent on Kingston the moment the ice leaves the lake. If he deems it practicable and you have troops enough to carry it, you will attempt the expedition.

Armstrong then enclosed a *false* set of orders, which he intended that Brown should let fall into the hands of the British in what Brown called a "ruse de guerre." They read:

> Public sentiment will no longer tolerate the possession of Fort Niagara by the enemy. You will therefore move the division which you have brought from French Mills and invest that post. General Tompkins will cooperate with you with 500 militia, and Colonel Scott, who is to be made a brigadier, will join you. You will receive your instructions at Onondago Hollow.

The intention was that this would induce Prevost and Drummond to send what men they could spare to the Niagara frontier, and Kingston would lie open to attack. But in an extraordinary misunderstanding, Brown decided that the false orders were in fact the real ones. He left a small garrison at Sackets Harbor, and marched off west, leaving an astonished Armstrong to

(Below) A contemporary view by E. E. Vidal of the Royal Navy squadron riding at anchor in Navy Bay, Kingston, in the spring of 1815. The ships have had their upper rigging removed, and on one of them the wooden roof set over the deck for the winter is still in place. The view is northward, with Point Henry to the right and Kingston harbour to the left.

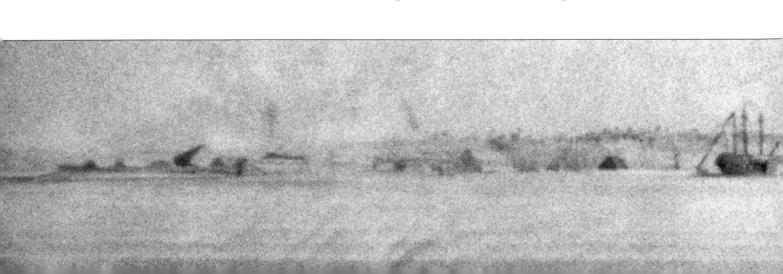

try and make the best of things. Armstrong's valid strategic sense of the importance of attacking Kingston and the St. Lawrence was now set aside by an unintended return to fighting on the Niagara frontier, which would not threaten Kingston or Montreal. In a letter to Brown, the bemused Armstrong tried to be philosophical:

> You have mistaken my meaning. . . . If on the other hand you left the Harbor with a competent force for its defence, go on and prosper. Good consequences are sometimes the result of mistakes.

Whether Kingston's defences of its batteries, garrison, and Yeo's ships might have fallen to a determined American attack is uncertain; what is certain is that Brown's real or calculated blunder ended for 1814 any serious threat to heartland Canada, and condemned both sides to a bloody summer of mutual slaughter on the Niagara frontier that threatened neither side with the loss of anything beyond military prestige.

When the news arrived at Kingston that Brown had trudged away to the west from Sackets Harbor, the incredulous Drummond and Yeo realized that an opportunity had been presented to attack either the naval base at Sackets Harbor or the supply transshipment point to Sackets that was at Oswego, New York – or both. Oswego was a former French trading post, built at the point where the Oswego River empties into Lake Ontario. It lay at the head of the water supply route from the Hudson and Mohawk valleys, by which Chauncey received his supplies. When the plan for an attack on these posts was presented to Sir George Prevost, he predictably was too cautious to accept the larger plan of attacking Sackets Harbor. Drummond's suggestion that the attack focus on the lightly defended Oswego won the day.

With some one thousand infantry packed into Yeo's ships, the force sailed from Kingston on May 4, 1814, standing out past Chauncey's old anchorage at Main Duck Island on the southerly track for Oswego. By early afternoon

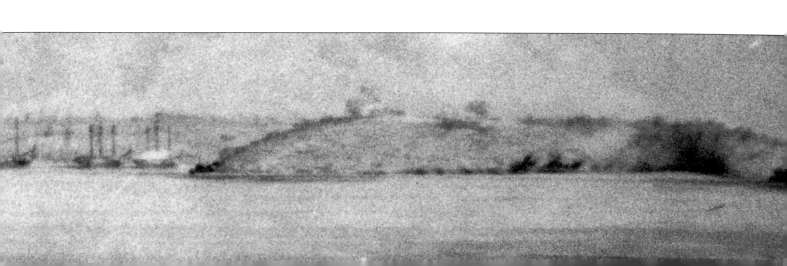

of the next day the squadron was tacking slowly back and forth off Oswego before a steady easterly wind.

On the eastern side of the long, narrow harbour there stood a fortification on a rise of land, Fort Ontario, and this held a garrison of three hundred American regular soldiery and a battery of six guns, under the command of a Colonel Mitchell, who also had access to a body of Oswego militia. Drummond was anxious to get ashore and undertake the assault, but Yeo's caution prevented a headlong landing that might have seized a known stockpile of American stores – including desperately needed flour – and overwhelmed Mitchell's three hundred regulars. Instead, Yeo repeated the interminable wait of the Sackets Harbor attack. Unlike Winfield Scott's lightning shore assault that had taken Fort George, Yeo sat off Oswego for an entire day and night, concerned about winds and shallows, while small boats methodically sounded the shoreline. This delay allowed the civilian population of Oswego to join the militiamen in working around the clock, carrying the naval and food supplies well out of reach up the Oswego River. Mitchell's call for help also brought militia flocking in from the countryside, raising his force to six hundred men.

A view, looking south from Lake Ontario, of Yeo's British squadron riding at anchor to an east wind, while ashore the British assault force, including the Canadian Glengarry Light Infantry, are attacking up the slope towards Fort Ontario at Oswego. Yeo's hesitancy about finding a safe anchorage allowed the Americans to move many of the naval stores upriver, safe from capture, before the assault.

Finally, on the following day, Yeo sent off the attack, having given Mitchell ample time to prepare. The boats suffered from the accurate gunnery of the fort as they pulled in through the brisk wind but, once ashore, the landing party of redcoats, Royal Marines, and Canadians of the Glengarry Light Infantry formed up on the slopes east of the fort and rushed it. The fight was over in minutes, but the regular American garrison retired soon enough to avoid capture, the militia at their heels. Drummond's men did manage to capture a thousand barrels of flour and a scuttled schooner, but missed the naval stores Chauncey needed to launch his ships and challenge Yeo. Had Yeo not been so cautious, he might have captured them, and so seized dominance of Lake Ontario for the summer of 1814.

Knowing he had missed the stores, Yeo took the landing force back to Kingston, then set out on May 19 to blockade Sackets Harbor in an effort to keep the supplies from reaching Chauncey. Chauncey had to risk shipping the stores, but determined to do it in small boats that would hug the shore from Oswego round to Sackets Harbor. To do this, Chauncey sent off the resourceful Melancthon Woolsey, who left Oswego on May 28 with nineteen boats laden with more than thirty ships' guns and mooring cables, rowed by seamen from Chauncey's squadron, and with an escort of green-clad riflemen. The flotilla crept along the Lake Ontario shoreline, rowing through the night, but on the next morning one of Yeo's patrolling ships spotted them and swooped in, capturing one boat. Woolsey had his men turn in to the mouth of Sandy Creek and row well up it.

A boat party from Yeo's squadron was sent in after them, under Commanders Francis Spilsbury and Stephen Popham, but when the British boats got well into the river they were caught in a devastating ambush set by Woolsey's sailors, the riflemen, and a party of Oneida warriors. The entire force surrendered, and at a stroke Yeo had lost two hundred prime seamen. Chauncey nonetheless decided to rely on new roads to get the remainder of his supplies to Sackets Harbor, and, in a demonstration of determination, some two hundred civilian volunteers carried the main cable for the new frigate *Superior*, then being built at Sackets, on their shoulders through the woods. Yeo's temporary advantage had vanished through hesitation and bad luck, and the stalemated building war on Lake Ontario resumed.

Drummond had called for the raids at the eastern end of Lake Ontario in the belief that Brown's march away had weakened the American strength threatening Kingston. But he had not fully realized that the main American strength was, illogically, gathering on the Niagara frontier. Drummond still believed that there was a strong army at Sackets Harbor, and that Chauncey would attack Kingston once his new ships were ready. At Fort George on the Niagara frontier, Phineas Riall would have to make do with the small force of regulars and militia he had on hand, a fact that did not disturb him unduly, for he, too, thought Brown was at Sackets Harbor – which was what common sense dictated.

Had Riall known what was happening on the far side of the Niagara River, he might have been less complacent. Brown was about to arrive at Buffalo and join his men to the brigade Winfield Scott had put together. Scott was a dedicated and painstaking officer, who was determined to overcome the lacklustre record of the regular United States Army against the British. Beginning with his officers and working down to the men, Scott instituted a Spartan regimen of discipline, drill, and training that put the men on the drill field for as long as ten hours a day, learning and practising the arts of steadiness, marching, volley firing, manoeuvre and crisp movement, and the myriad skills that had turned their counterparts in the British infantry into some of the world's best. Short of uniform cloth, Scott's brigade wore a simple, unlaced grey coat that suggested well the austere professionalism he was determined to instill. By the time the fighting season of early summer arrived, and with it Armstrong's orders to make the best of Brown's mistake, Brown had a formidable force waiting at Buffalo, of which Scott's brigade was the brightly honed leading edge.

Armstrong's orders in hand, "Smuggler" Brown considered his objectives. He was to ignore Fort George and Fort Erie, unless they could be easily taken, and cross diagonally northwest over the Niagara Peninsula to capture Burlington. Cutting Riall's supply route and leaving him to starve on the Niagara frontier, the force would then be transported by Chauncey to Kingston for a climactic assault on that place.

The plan began to unfold on July 3, 1814, when Winfield Scott led the first of three brigades across the Niagara River, crossing at midnight without the loss of a man. The second and third brigades, under Eleazer Ripley and Peter B. Porter, followed the next morning, and by noon Brown had his army ashore. The force deployed in front of Fort Erie, where the commander, Major Thomas Buck of the 8th (King's) Regiment, had 150 men to resist Brown's 3,500. Buck surrendered, and Brown turned to move north along the river-edge road. To keep Riall occupied, American militiamen at Lewiston, New York, manoeuvred as if to attack Fort Niagara or cross the river at Queenston. Meanwhile, Brown marched at a quick pace, anxious to take his next objective, the British staging point at Chippewa, on the Chippewa River just above Niagara Falls.

Word of the landing had reached Riall at Fort George early in the morning, and he repeated Brock's fateful ride, galloping south after ordering every available man to be marched towards Chippewa, even ordering back the companies of the 8th (King's) who had been sent off to York to rest. By nightfall on July 4, Riall had a heterogeneous force of regulars, militia, and warriors, with some artillery, behind rough entrenchments on the north side of the Chippewa River. On the south side, perhaps a half mile away, the most advanced of the three American brigades – Scott's – had encamped.

Scott had narrowly missed being taken prisoner when the Canadian farmhouse where he took breakfast was approached by a party of Riall's warriors. Scott galloped back to his camp with the warriors whooping behind him, and the warriors and some accompanying Canadian militia pursued him right to his camp, skirmishing with his sentries. Porter was informed, and he sent forward a party of woodsmen from Pennsylvania, who dispersed the Canadians and warriors.

Scott was preparing to stage a previously planned full-dress review of his command – his nickname throughout his army career was "Old Fuss and Feathers" – when word arrived that the warriors had not been an isolated raiding party, but that behind it a large British column had crossed the Chippewa and outflanked Porter's men, and was coming on, threatening from the north. Riall had decided to move. As Porter's Pennsylvanians came rushing back in a lather to the rear, Scott advanced his parade-ready brigade to the broad stretch of fields that lay between Street's Creek, just to the south of the Chippewa River, and the Chippewa itself. Here he deployed into line, dressed his ranks, and had his men prime and load their long French-style muskets, and wait.

In front of Scott, Riall pushed his column forward, the scampering retreat of the Pennsylvanians reassuring him that he was facing a mere militia horde. That impression was sustained as he came into view of the silent line waiting for him, dressed in more of the simple grey militia homespun. But then, as Riall approached, Scott manoeuvred his brigade and Riall noted his mistake too late, breathing, "Those are *regulars*, by God!" as he saw the grey ranks move in steady precision. The battle was about to be joined, and, in an ironic reversal, the Americans stood in a thin, two-rank line of

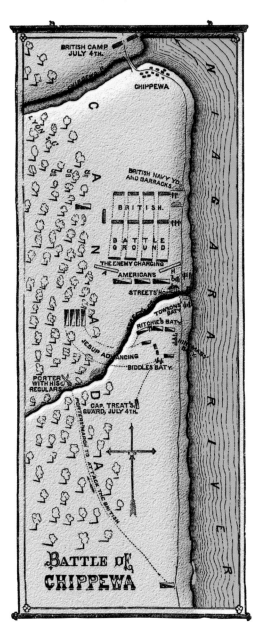

This plan of the Battle of Chippewa, July 1814, shows the disposition of the opposing troops. Winfield Scott's brigade held the centre of the American line against Riall's advance.

At Chippewa, British com-mander Phineas Riall was deceived by the grey homespun coats worn by Scott's brigade, into thinking he was about to engage American militia. The steady discipline and manoeu-vring of Scott's men under heavy British fire led Riall to exclaim in surprise, "Those are regulars, by God!" The makeshift grey uniform of Scott's force is perpetuated in the dress uniform of the United States Military Academy at West Point to this day.

the type so favoured by the British infantry, while Riall had his British and Canadians advancing in French-style columns, of which only the men in the leading files could engage their muskets. It was a formation that might have brushed aside militia, but Scott's brigade was anything but that.

The British and Canadians came on with steady discipline, but Scott responded with a classic manoeuvre. He pulled back the centre of his line and advanced either wing, like the horns of a steer, pinioning his prey. As the British columns entered musket range, Scott unleashed a series of thunderclap volleys. The British columns halted and gradually disintegrated, regimental groups clumping together in the thick fog of smoke, and fighting individually rather than as a cohesive line. Scott's brigade remained steady, and finally Riall broke off the attack and retired from the field, the humiliated general being one of the last men to leave. It had been an unequivocal American victory, and Scott's brigade had served notice that the comic-opera performance of American regular soldiery had come to an end. Had this kind of victory been

won at Kingston instead of on the relatively remote Niagara frontier, Sir George Prevost in Quebec would have had grounds for worry indeed.

The casualty figures for Chippewa spoke of a new, terrible efficiency to the fighting. The British had lost more than 350 men killed or wounded, with more missing and presumed captured, while Scott's tightly arrayed ranks had suffered more than 300 killed, wounded, or missing. With less and less real chance for victory, the war was becoming a toe-to-toe killing contest between equally matched British, Canadians, and Americans.

Now Drummond had to admit to a defeat in open battle, but he was not prepared to withdraw from the Niagara Peninsula. Instead Riall was ordered to retire northward, which he did, cautiously pursued by

An imaginative but inaccurate American view of the Battle of Chippewa gives a good idea of the close nature of fighting in the era of the flintlock musket. The obligatory buckskinned militiaman shown on the left was rarely a participant in such set-piece battles as Lundy's Lane, Chippewa, or Crysler's Farm.

Brown's army. Not stopping at Queenston – where Brown thought he would fight – Riall withdrew all the way to Fort George.

Now Brown found himself in a difficult situation. Ideally, he was to push to Burlington and ignore Fort George. But Riall could then issue out and cut the supply line back to Buffalo that Brown was laboriously maintaining. For Brown the solution was Chauncey's fleet, which would both carry supplies and help in taking Fort George. Waiting at Queenston as had been agreed, Brown looked in vain for Chauncey's sails on the lake, finally sending off a desperate note to Sackets Harbor on July 13:

All accounts agree that the force of the enemy at Kingston is very light. Meet me on the lake shore north of Fort George with your fleet and we will be able I have no doubt to settle a plan of operations that will break the power of the enemy in the Canadas. . . . At all events let me hear from you. I have looked for your fleet with the greatest anxiety since the 10th. I do not doubt my ability to meet the enemy in the field and march in any direction over his country, your fleet carrying for me the necessary supplies. We can threaten Fort George and Niagara, and carry Burlington Heights and York, and proceed to Kingston and carry that place. For God's sake let me see you. Sir James will not fight. Two of his vessels are now in the Niagara River. If you conclude to meet me at the head of the lake have the goodness to bring the guns and troops that I have ordered from Sackett's [sic] Harbor.

It was another key moment, when fortune once again favoured the American plan of conquest – had cooperation and conjunction been possible. But Chauncey did not arrive, and eventually Brown had to realize that Chauncey was preoccupied with Yeo, and would stick to the plan he had laid out to Brown in a June 25 letter:

If Sir James pursues the policy that he did last Year of avoiding a general action I should be obliged to watch his movements to prevent his doing mischief. I shall therefore be governed by circumstances if he visits the head of the lake with his fleet you may expect to see me there also if he returns to Kingston I shall remain in this vicinity to watch his movements.

In other words, unless Yeo emerged from Kingston, Brown would have no support from Chauncey, regardless of what Brown intended.

A kind of pause now occurred, with Brown settling into a camp at Queenston to digest his situation, and Riall removing himself along the Lake Ontario shore to Twenty Mile Creek – the modern St. Catharines – to be ready to counter a march by Brown against either Fort George or Burlington Heights. Riall's force grew as militiamen came in, and meanwhile Brown's irregular forces repeated the pattern set by George McClure's militia, looting and burning the countryside at will in the area Brown controlled. Brown tried to counter it – sacking the officer who condoned the burning of the little village of St. David's

To land observers, the reluctance of Yeo and Chauncey to risk a fateful confrontation on Lake Ontario produced naval encounters that seemed more like yacht races than battles, with one side or the other appearing to run away. In September 1813, Chauncey's vessels – shown at the top in this sketch by American midshipman Peter Spicer – pursued Yeo's ships from the mouth of the Genesee River to the False Duck Islands and Prince Edward Bay on the Canadian shore.

– but it was a losing process, and the looting much disturbed the regular American officers. One, speaking of the American militia and their renegade Canadian henchmen, said that they had "plundered and burnt everything. The whole population is against us. . . ." It was a shameful return to the depredations of 1813, and it deepened the enmity of the fighting.

Faced with Chauncey's refusal to cooperate, Brown called a council of war at Queenston, and at first was inclined to follow the suggestion of Winfield Scott, who was all for assaulting Forts Niagara and George to secure an anchorage for Chauncey. Then news came that large reinforcements had arrived with Riall at Twenty Mile Creek. It was an inaccurate report, but with it came a cold note from Chauncey telling Brown that "we are intended to seek and fight the enemy's fleet and I shall not be diverted from my efforts to effect it by any sinister attempt to render us subordinate to, or an appendage of, the army." What Brown thought of that dismissal is not recorded, but it made up his mind. He packed up the Queenston camp and moved it south to the battlefield at Chippewa, settling in there on July 24, 1814, to watch and wait to see what Riall would think of next. There was very little Brown could do, given the collapse of the grand design. But at least his supply route to Buffalo would be secure. It was as he set up his tent rows and posted his sentries that Brown at last received the news of Napoleon's final defeat, and his banishment to Elba, and he realized that hardened British regulars in their thousands were en route to Canada. Was Riall even now receiving some of them? It was a grim prospect.

What Brown did not know was that Wellington's veterans were indeed already coming off the ships in Quebec, but Prevost had intentions of using them in another way. Riall, and Drummond behind him, would fight Brown with the increasingly exhausted mix of redcoats and Canadian militia he had faced at Chippewa. He would soon find out, however, that Riall was nonetheless prepared to carry the war to him. The stage was about to be set for the battle that most symbolized the futile waste and courageous obstinacy that characterized so much of the war.

Phineas Riall was nothing if not brave, and he determined to try and cut off Brown's force as it retired, assuming it would continue as far as Fort Erie. On the hot, still night of July 24, Riall set out with a force of just under a thousand redcoats and militia, marching in a roundabout way to reach the river-edge cart track at about the point of the falls themselves. As day came, the troops emerged finally on an east-west cartway called Lundy's Lane, and halted there almost within earshot of the thunder of the falls. Behind them, at Ten Mile Creek, another thousand men were preparing to set out on the march south. Three miles to the south of where Riall's advance had stopped, Brown's army was stirring in its tents at Chippewa, and had just received news that British troops were on the march. But the troops referred to were not Riall's.

On July 24, several of Sir James Yeo's ships had arrived at York with red-coat reinforcements, catching up there with others who had been marching dustily around the lake by road from Kingston after the news of the Chippewa loss had reached Kingston. (Yeo's ships had been held in Kingston by adverse winds.) These troops and Drummond were now carried over to the mouth of the Niagara, where Drummond learned that Brown had retired and Riall was off in hot pursuit. Drummond marched south down the river, leaving some detachments at Queenston, unaware of Riall's precise location and unaware too that Riall had another force inland that was also marching south. By noon, Brown in his camp had received a garbled message that British forces were coming south on both sides of the river, and one of these could be caught at Queenston.

When no clarifying information arrived, Brown ordered Scott's brigade to return towards Queenston, in the late afternoon of July 25. The heat was stifling, and the men were soon coated in white dust as they tramped northward. Pausing by chance just south of the falls, Scott heard surprising news: a British force was just a little more than a mile ahead, where Lundy's Lane joined the coastal road. Scott sent a messenger flying back to Brown, then deployed his column into line and approached the British position, which occupied the top of a low rise of ground in the cleared fields.

Riall's force was preponderantly militia, with some four hundred Canadian regulars and a few dragoons. When he saw the familiar long grey line appear again, his prudence came to the fore, and he began to withdraw, sending a messenger off to find his second force and order them to do the same. No sooner had Riall commenced the march, however, than he spotted a dust cloud in the distance, which revealed itself to be Drummond's column marching south. Although it was late in the day and Drummond

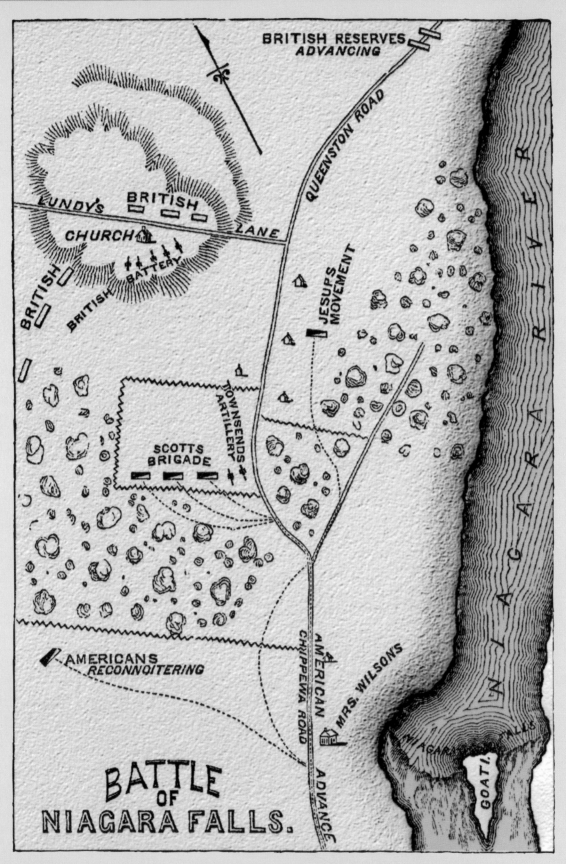

BATTLE
OF
NIAGARA FALLS.

The disposition of the opposing armies in 1814 just before the commencement of the clash that Benjamin Lossing, writing forty years later, would refer to as the Battle of Niagara Falls, but which is now known as the Battle of Lundy's Lane. Winfield Scott's brigade, shown deploying in the centre of the diagram, suffered heavy losses, with Scott himself being wounded.

A CHANGING IMAGE: THE BLOODY STALEMATE AT LUNDY'S LANE

The Battle of Lundy's Lane was a bloody and savage encounter in which British and Canadian troops fought the Americans to a draw in the stifling heat and darkness of a midsummer night. The changing portrayals of the event reflect the outlook and ideals of the ages in which the images were produced. The contemporary image of the battle (top) observes conventions of the time, in which the figures are drawn with great simplicity, and the lines of troops are shown moving in the meticulous unison that was the ideal rather than the reality. The second work (below left), done many decades later by Alonzo Chappel, takes a Victorian glory in romantic, individual posturing and elaborate uniforms, and suggests the battle was fought in daylight. The third work, by C. W. Jefferys in the modern era, is a return to greater accuracy of dress and equipment, but seeks as well to show the gritty horror of the fighting, lit by the lurid flashes of gunfire, and the bitter resolution shown by both sides not to give in as the slaughter went on.

now had a little under two thousand men, he ordered Riall's men to join the column; he would continue to push on south.

Soon they came in sight of Scott's brigade, which had halted just short of the low rise. Drummond deployed into line and advanced to the top of the rise, placing his guns in the centre. In the blazing orange light of the late afternoon, the two armies stood in sweaty silence, eyeing one another. Then, just after 6:oo p.m., Scott made the first move. The cry rang out, "To the front, march!" and Scott's grey line advanced in beautiful formation on the British and Canadians. But this time the defenders stood fast in their own long, motionless line, watching the American come on, hearing the clink and rattle of the enemy's kit above their own breathing, waiting, waiting. . . .

The order to fire came suddenly, and a sharp volley burst from the British line in a rippling pink flash, then another, the men biting the cartridges in a fever, priming and then ramming home the charges with clinking ramrods to fire again, until the air before them was opaque with smoke. Scott's brigade wavered, the grey-clad bodies falling in heaps, and now Scott was down too, wounded, the air full of the shrieks of injured men and the cries of the sergeants and officers to dress the line, to keep the advance steady. But the British and Canadians were not going to yield this time, and the punishing volleys were finally too much. Brown pulled Scott's shattered brigade back and placed it in reserve, preparing to advance Eleazer Ripley's men against the unmoving line of red on the low rise and to send Porter's Pennsylvanians to try and get round the British right flank. A pause occurred, and the men on both sides stood running with sweat.

Then the battle began again. A small flanking party of Americans had succeeded in getting around the British line on the river's edge and briefly captured a wounded Riall before being shattered in a rush of British bayonets. By now darkness had settled over the site. A moon rode, orange and bloated, in the hot night sky that suddenly was lit again by pink flashes as Ripley's men came on, and the British and Canadians responded. The formations closed to where men could hear orders being given in the enemy ranks, and the world became a nightmarish chaos of volleys and cannon blasts, shouted orders, the screams of wounded men, hoarse cries of encouragement or despair. The lines rippled and surged towards one another, bayonets clashing in the cloaking, smoky murk.

Slowly, Brown's men began to get the upper hand, and the knoll of the hill, the road junction, and now the British guns were in their possession. But at that point Riall's reserve force arrived, dusty and parched after their march from Lake Ontario. A few blundered into Americans in the dark, and were lost, but the rest Drummond thrust into his tattered line, forming them all once more, ordering the newcomers to fix bayonets. Then, with a cry, Drummond launched them up the knoll again at the panting American line. Volleys banged out, and redcoats fell kicking in the dirt, but still the bayonet line came on; now it was the American line that was stumbling back down the slope of the knoll, dragging away captured British guns, leaving one of theirs. By this time both armies could barely stay on their feet, and both were suffering horribly from the heat and the raging thirst that black powder brings on, their faces those of dark spectres in the gun flashes. The firing ceased, the silence broken only by the men's heavy breathing and the dreadful sounds coming from the stirring heaps of wounded.

The ghastly effects of cannon fire and the impact of heavy lead musket balls were captured in Napoleonic-era drawings by British Army physician Charles Bell. Men suffering wounds of this nature as often died of shock as from the gangrene and infection that invariably set in.

The survivors stared at one another through the darkness, the sweat stinging down their temples from under the shakos, the hot air burning their lungs. Neither side would yield. Neither side had displayed anything but a dogged courage that only added poignancy to the terrible casualty toll of the dead or writhing injured. The "butcher's bill" was heavy: Brown and Scott, both wounded; Riall and Drummond, both wounded; among the British and Canadians, 878 men killed, wounded, or missing; among the Americans, 853 men killed, wounded, or missing.

Brown's injury forced him from the field, but he left orders to retire only to the camp at Chippewa and return the next day if the British awaited another struggle. The command went to Ripley, and he did not return to the field, evacuating his camp the next day and retiring instead to Fort Erie. The British and Canadians slept in agonized exhaustion on the battlefield. They had not triumphed, but they had not lost. The Americans would not have their conquest in 1814, as they had not in 1812 and 1813. But it would not be for lack of courage in the grey-and-blue ranks that closed time and again with the redcoats, who matched them with every blow.

Drummond, though wounded, was determined to press after the enemy. As soon as his men were able to move, he marched south in pursuit of Ripley. The latter had not wasted time when he arrived at Fort Erie on August 3, but threw his men into work parties that turned the incomplete fort into a menacing stronghold of log ramparts, earthworks, and gun embrasures, out of which thirteen guns projected, their fire supported by the broadsides of three United States Navy vessels anchored just offshore in a protective line. To assault this impressive position, Drummond had slightly more than three thousand men, including some sailors who promptly "cut out" two of the anchored ships, the *Somers* and the *Ohio.*

The man on the left had been blinded by a musket ball that passed through both his eyes; the man on the right had his cheek pierced by a ball. It was the American custom to load muskets with smaller "buckshot" as well as ball, to make them more lethal.

The nut of the fortification would be a far more difficult thing to crack. Drummond had no suitable artillery, but he ordered his small battery of guns to begin banging away at the fort on August 12, to little effect. Finally, with impetuosity getting the better of prudence, Drummond ordered an assault on the place after three days of the "bombardment." It was to prove a costly decision. Drummond decided to attack the fort at three points: an outlying redoubt called Snake Hill, the central fort itself, and a water-edge battery of guns.

The attack went in at 2:00 a.m. on the morning of August 15, and immediately ran into difficulties when the thirteen hundred men ordered to take Snake Hill with the bayonet found their scaling ladders had been made too short. After five separate attempts to somehow get into the redoubt, they were driven back with heavy casualties. The force sent against the water-edge battery was repulsed similarly. Only the force that had gone against the older, central part of the fort had any success, when the British and Canadians entered the old bastion, cramming in until almost five hundred men were inside. Just as morning light illuminated the scene, however, the powder magazine in the old bastion went up in a horrendous explosion, killing or wounding nearly all the attackers. Drummond's force withdrew to

lick its wounds, and the casualty toll was taken. For an American loss of 84 men, Drummond had suffered the appalling loss of 905 men killed, wounded, missing, or taken prisoner. It was evident nothing but a long and deliberate siege would take Fort Erie.

That said, Drummond found the siege anything but easy to mount. The weather had begun to cool towards fall and had become miserably rainy. Sickness appeared in the British camp among the squalid huts and the rows of mildewed tents. Drummond received a few hundred men from Prevost, eked out of the massive force that was assembling in Lower Canada, but he had to send others off to Burlington and Fort George to recover from wounds or illness. He began to improve the bombardment batteries, expanding them from one to four and laboriously dragging guns down from Fort George to make the cannonading significant. Drummond was not about to let go.

Jacob Brown had recovered quickly from his wounds and taken command again at Fort Erie, increasingly concerned that he would be driven out of it. The grand plan to sweep down the lake and river to Montreal was a memory, and now Brown had to face a determined siege from Drummond, all the while knowing that the British troops were pouring ashore at Quebec. He appealed to Secretary of War Armstrong in Washington, and to George Izard at Plattsburg, for help.

When John Armstrong received this plea, however, he was dealing with other disturbing realities: the Royal Navy was roaming destructively up Chesapeake Bay and along the coast of Maine; Sir George Prevost at Quebec was being presented with a massive army of European veterans, and clearly would be doing something with them. Armstrong's most logical action would have been to focus what defences he had on dealing with the British forces on the coast, and to prepare Izard to meet an almost-certain

An 1841 American rendering of the fateful British attack on Fort Erie by Drummond on the night of August 13, 1814. Two parts of a three-part British attack had been repulsed, but a third part, under command of General Drummond's nephew William Drummond, succeeded in getting into a main bastion of the fort before the detonation of a magazine below them shattered the attack, killing most of the assaulting force.

southern thrust from Prevost. But with War Hawk politicians still assailing him over the importance of the war against Canada on the western frontier, Armstrong did neither, and George Izard at Plattsburg was astonished to find himself ordered to march with most of his five thousand troops west to support Brown at Fort Erie. On August 29, 1814, he set off, his progress helped in part by Isaac Chauncey's temporary superiority in the shipbuilding war on Lake Ontario.

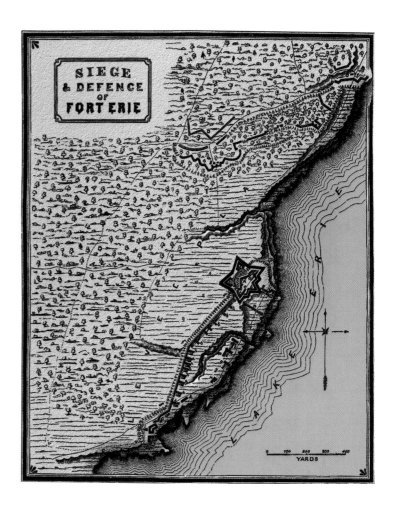

In Fort Erie, Brown was not about to go down without a fight. On September 15, he sent out two columns of men under Peter Porter and James Miller to attack the four British bombardment batteries. Covered by the incessant rain that had begun to produce dysentery and fever in the troops on both sides, Porter and Miller rushed the British positions and managed to take two of the batteries, spiking the guns, only to then be furiously counterattacked by the British. It was their first contact with Wellington's veterans, and the Americans lost more than a third of their number in an unequal bayonet contest before managing to escape back to the fort. On the other hand, although Drummond had not lost, the loss of more than six hundred men in the attack was too harsh a blow to bear. The siege could not succeed on these terms.

Leaving his encampment intact to deceive the Americans, Drummond formed up his sodden ranks and trudged morosely away with them in the rain on September 21, intent on re-establishing himself at the Chippewa camp and awaiting his fate. He had learned of Izard's march, and assumed Chauncey still dominated Lake Ontario, which meant Fort George was at risk. As Drummond

When Brown retired into Fort Erie after Lundy's Lane, he set about improving its defences, so that Drummond had to face a formidable fortification. The defences at Snake Hill, at the bottom of the diagram, were the scene of a bloody attempt by Drummond to carry the fortifications by assault.

FORT ERIE BASTION BLOWN UP.

A depiction of the explosion in the bastion of Fort Erie that shattered Drummond's attacking force and ended any serious attempt by the British to take the fort. The British later withdrew northwards to Chippewa, and the Americans abandoned the fort, destroying it as they left.

squelched into Chippewa, he was unaware that the fortunes of war were about to shift again.

George Izard had arrived on the Niagara frontier after a month's march, and now took over from Jacob Brown. He immediately crossed to the Canadian shore on October 11 and moved slowly north after Drummond, whom Izard now outnumbered, 8,000 men to 2,500. But Izard was about to receive some startling news. He had just established his camp at Street's Creek, within view of the bloody battlefield at Lundy's Lane, when a despatch arrived to inform him that Chauncey was, abruptly, no longer in control of Lake Ontario. Sir James Yeo at Kingston had launched a huge, first-rate ship of the line, *Saint Lawrence*, which boasted more than a hundred guns, and Chauncey's squadron was now at Sackets Harbor, sheltering under shore defences.

Izard had grave doubts about taking his force north and east, despite the fact that his troops outnumbered Drummond's, and he wrote to Armstrong on October 16 expressing his concern:

This defeats all the objects of the operations by land in this quarter. I may turn Chippawa, and, should General Drummond not retire, may succeed in giving him a great deal of trouble, but if he falls back on Fort George or Burlington Heights, every step I take in pursuit exposes me to be cut off by the large reinforcements it is . . . in the power of the enemy to throw in twenty-four hours upon my flank or rear.

Izard gloomily contemplated Drummond's camp ahead of him. The Canadian had busied his redcoats and militia with spade and axe, and Chippewa had more the look of a fort than a simple camp. If he was about to be defeated, Drummond was going to make it costly. Izard probed the possibilities of outflanking him by sending a force of 1,500 men off to the west to find a way behind Drummond, but Drummond countered with a blocking force of 750 men. They clashed at Cook's Mills,

Lake Ontario Patrol, 1814, by Peter Rindlisbacher. By 1814 both the British and the Americans were operating navies on Lake Ontario of a size and strength that would have been inconceivable in 1812. Yeo's new flagship Saint Lawrence, *launched in 1814, was larger than Nelson's* Victory *and could mount a broadside of up to 112 guns, while at Sackets Harbor, Chauncey was building a 120-gun monster, eventually named the* New Orleans. *Afraid of losing a conclusive engagement, their commanders kept the fleets from ever engaging in a decisive contest.*

about ten miles from the Niagara shore, and the Americans got the worst of the struggle in the rain before contact was broken off. The American commander reported the resistance to Izard, and Izard decided to risk his forces no further. Drummond was evidently dug in and had an unspecified number of men, and Yeo was in command of the lake, presumably preparing to ship yet more veteran redcoats up to Drummond. Izard abruptly broke camp, and retired to Fort Erie. There, he mined the fortifications, and on November 5 a series of blasts and explosions destroyed the fort. British and Canadian patrols arrived in time to find the walls destroyed, the buildings ablaze, and Izard's army gone to winter quarters in Buffalo.

It was the end of the campaign – and of the war on the Niagara frontier. Izard's departure left only the small American garrison at Fort Malden on the Detroit frontier as an American presence on Canadian soil. There was little to show for two years of savage, fruitless war, beyond the burial mounds of thousands of young men and the smoking ruins of Canadian and American farms and villages. Drummond's men sat and watched the endless rain fall. They would spend the winter at Fort George, or York.

When asked about a solution to the war with the United States, the Duke of Wellington would only observe that control of the Great Lakes was vital to succeeding in the defence of Canada – but that the Americans were, for all practical purposes, unconquerable.

To the east, in the historic invasion corridor of the Lake Champlain–Richelieu River Valley, another fateful drama was played out over the summer and fall, as Riall, Drummond, Scott, and Brown fought to their valorous and bloody stalemate on the Niagara frontier. It had been in early May that, Napoleon defeated, the British government had turned its attention to the war in North America. When the Duke of Wellington was approached to lead the effort, he managed to avoid the appointment, observing only that command of the lakes was key to the defence of Canada, and that the United States was, for all practical purposes, unconquerable. The British knew that Madison's emissaries at Ghent were to be negotiating an end to the war, not its continuance. It would have given the British a sizeable advantage if the United States could be dealt a military blow, and even a territorial loss, that would enhance the British negotiating position.

A kind of plan developed. In it, a major British amphibious force, based at Bermuda, would attack the eastern seaboard of the United States. A force from Halifax would occupy the northern portion of Maine, to see if the difficult line of the border could be adjusted in Britain's favour. Inland, Sir George Prevost was to take the relatively enormous force of twelve thousand men being sent to him, and take as well the suggestion from Lord Bathurst that he carry out the "entire destruction of Sackets Harbor and the Naval establishment on Lake Erie and Lake Champlain."

If Isaac Brock had lived to this moment, the prospect of what he, or even a Gordon Drummond, might have done with such a force invites speculation. But Sir George was venturing into waters in which he swam poorly. His personality and inclination had suited him to the careful husbandry of resources and extreme caution the precarious defence of the Canadas demanded – in some eyes; now he was called upon to lay aside the administrator's pen and take up the sword, and at Sackets Harbor and elsewhere Prevost had not shown the ability to distinguish between due prudence and a fatal reluctance to simply fight. Events now conspired to focus on this aspect of his character. But if Prevost saw only a Burgoyne-like doom awaiting him, his daughter Anne saw only glowing promise:

> I was most sanguine that something very brilliant would be achieved. I had often thought with regret that my Father had never yet been engaged in any bright affair – he had considered it necessary to conduct the defence of the Canadas with much caution, – defence, not conquest, was necessarily his object. But now I thought the time had arrived when all murmurs would be silenced – I was delighted to think my Father was commanding some thousands of Wellington's soldiers! . . . O how high the pulse of hope beat at that moment. I do not recollect that I had any sort of fear as to the result of the Expedition. I looked forward to certain victory.
>
> – *Journal of Anne Prevost, later addition to entry of August 30, 1814*

Anne Prevost had a daughter's faith in her father. Sir George Prevost himself was not as enthusiastic about what he was undertaking – he had chosen

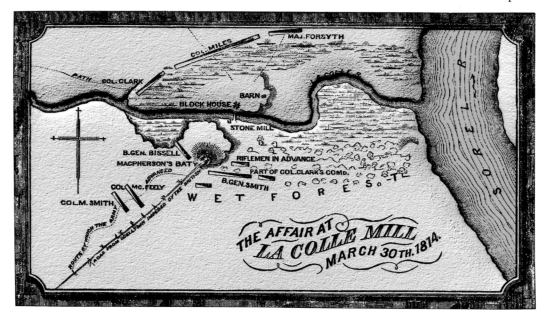

At Lacolle, in 1814, a confused attack by an American force that had come north from Plattsburg was repulsed with few casualties. This failure effectively ended the military career of James Wilkinson, who, after calling off the descent of the St. Lawrence, had put his troops into winter camp at French Mills (now Fort Covington, New York) and then Plattsburg. The defeat at Lacolle marked the end of American incursions into Lower Canada.

to attack Plattsburg – and as he marched his long columns of toughened regulars out from Montreal in the hot August sun, heading towards the American border, his misgivings were more in evidence than his eagerness to strike at the enemy. His force was a balanced one, well supplied with artillery and stores, and at a size of three divisions of twelve thousand men it would have had little trouble striking as deep as Albany if its supply route could be maintained. As for the matter of naval support from the squadron at Ile aux Noix on the Richelieu, Prevost had relied on Sir James Yeo to ensure it, and the state of that squadron was not encouraging.

Drummond and Yeo had attempted to convince Prevost to turn the huge army against Sackets Harbor, but Prevost would not listen to their entreaties – which mirrored Bathurst's orders – and instead had decided for a cautious strike at the closest of targets, Plattsburg. Wilkinson had made a last, feeble thrust north to Lacolle in March 1814, and had been replaced by Izard when that failed. When Prevost's column moved across the border on September 1, the bizarre westward march of George Izard to the Niagara frontier had reduced the Plattsburg garrison, under Alexander Macomb, to three thousand men, a goodly portion of whom were untried militia. Prevost's juggernaut could roll easily over them, provided a general of Wellington's character was present. Prevost, however, was to prove no Wellington.

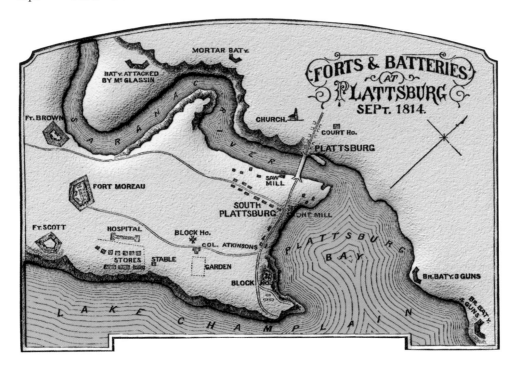

Prevost had designed a plan that called for a joint attack on the New York town. Macdonough had brought his naval squadron over from Burlington and anchored it in Plattsburg Bay as floating batteries positioned to support Macomb's land defence or repel an attack from the lake. Prevost's plan called for the Ile aux Noix squadron to defeat Macdonough, while Prevost assaulted Macomb's defences from the landward side. Already, however, Prevost was displaying a hesitancy that at first astonished his veteran senior officers. Soon their feelings turned to something close to contempt as Prevost inched the columns towards Plattsburg in the face of negligible resistance, rather than making a lightning march south.

On his flank, the naval squadron at Ile aux Noix, after months of inattention and poor supply from Yeo, grappled with the need to prepare itself hurriedly for an engagement with a well-supplied and well-led enemy. The commander at Ile aux Noix's shipyard, Captain Peter Fisher, had set his few sailors and shipwrights to work frantically attempting to prepare the ships and to launch the frigate *Confiance*, 37 guns, which did not slide into the water until August 25. Fisher would not lead the squadron south, however. On September 2 Captain George Downie arrived from Kingston with orders from Yeo to get the squadron under way. By September 9, after a

The defensive positions at the village of Plattsburg, New York, in September 1814. Prevost approached from the north with his huge force and halted along the Saranac River. The Americans had ordered away many of their defending troops to the Niagara frontier, and Prevost faced a small garrison that would have been quickly overcome had he made any serious attempt at an attack.

pell-mell that caused many sleepless nights, with the ships still coated with sawdust and volunteer crews only half aware of their tasks, he reported to Prevost that he could sail.

Since September 6 Prevost had been halted north of Plattsburg waiting for this news, which he had goaded out of Downie with thinly masked disparaging comments about naval readiness. Now Prevost crawled south, while Downie's ships worked their way into the lake with no sign of enemy vessels. Prevost's advance brushed aside an advance defence position commanded by a General Mooers – his veterans not even bothering to deploy out of column – and finally arrived outside Plattsburg. There he could see that Macomb had built a fortified position on the far bank of the Saranac River, but one that Prevost's force could have overwhelmed in a few hours of sharp fighting. Again, however, Prevost held back his force, turning them instead to several days of unnecessary entrenching work, while he sent off a letter to Downie. In it, he ordered Downie to attack Macdonough, while he would assault Macomb "at nearly the same time." Had Prevost actually done so, and turned Macomb's guns and his own against Macdonough's ships, the coming naval battle might have had a different result.

On the morning of September 11, in a light wind, Downie rounded the point that opened into Plattsburg Bay, firing guns to alert Prevost that the plan was under way. Now was the time for Prevost to hurl his superior force against Macomb, but he chose to sit immobile as Downie sailed in, unsupported, to meet a very well-prepared Thomas Macdonough. Macdonough had anchored his fleet in a semi-circular line, with spring lines run to his anchor cables that allowed each ship to pivot and direct its broadside fire. With no threat from the shore, Macdonough packed his gun crews at the seaward guns, and awaited Downie. The British vessels closed with him in customary direct-ness, and a murderous, close-range naval battle ensued, in which

A plan of the naval battle off Plattsburg in the last moments. Macdonough had anchored his squadron across the channel between Cumberland Head and Crab Island, to serve as floating gun platforms. Downie's British squadron approached from the open lake, and its attack was to be the signal for a land attack by Prevost. Prevost failed to support Downie, and Macdonough, his ships unhampered by British fire from shore, hammered Downie's squadron into submission.

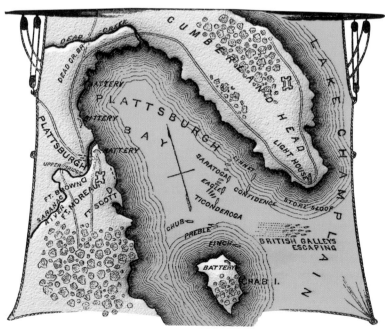

*A compressed contemporary view of the Battle of Plattsburg, with British and American
units engaging in the foreground while the rival naval squadrons grapple in the distance.*

Macdonough defeated Downie in a few hours filled with courage and tenacious fighting on both sides. When it ended, Daniel Pring, who had done so much to build the squadron, was the last officer on his feet able to pull down the colours. Downie was dead aboard his stricken *Confiance*, both squadrons were shattered hulks full of dead and wounded, and Thomas Macdonough had won for the United States Navy a bloody and hard-fought victory.

Prevost had held his troops back for hours, to their dismayed fury, finally releasing them to attack only when victory was in Macdonough's hands. His troops had just begun the assault when word came that Pring had struck his colours, and, if Prevost had been slow to give the order to attack, he was lightning quick in issuing a recall order that stopped the attack almost before it began. His incredulous brigadiers were stunned to receive an order directing them to abandon the attack altogether and retire to the Canadas. He was unmoved by their anger, writing later to Lord Bathurst that he did so "because the most complete success would have been unavailing, and the possession of the Enemy's works offered no advantage to compensate for the loss we must have sustained in acquiring Possession of them." Prevost did not seem to realize that his task had been to *obtain* advantage for his government, and he had been given a singularly powerful tool with which to do so. And he had failed. The import was not lost on the young Anne Prevost:

> The mortifying news arrived that our Squadron was defeated, captured, and Captain Downie killed. The scene of our hearing the news is now before me. Mr. Brenton came into the drawing-room much agitated and told us first the sad fate of our little Fleet which was, by the way, quite as large as the American squadron. I was breathless till I heard what the Army was about; the loss of the Fleet seemed to me a secondary consideration, and when Mr. B. went on to say the Army is in retreat, it seemed to me I heard a death's knell ringing in my ears. . . .
> I felt certain that however necessary this determination might be, it would bring the greatest Odium on my father – it would not be tolerated at a period especially when our troops were so perpetually victorious. O how my heart ached that day, and often, often afterwards!
> – *Journal of Anne Prevost, later addition to entry for September 12, 1814*

Prevost recoiled homeward, the jeers of his soldiery almost audible, the tragedy unfolding about him as he took the wasted army back to Montreal. Now had been his moment of crisis, like Brock and Tecumseh before him. To them, the enemy lay before them, and their warrior bravery carried them into the attack. In so doing they won admiration and honour, but also death and defeat. This had been Prevost's moment, when his endless prudence and hesitancy could have been transformed into triumph, a living triumph greater than one bought by death – if only he had known that the moment had arrived to set aside caution and commit, at last, to the attack. But the moment passed, and his career and reputation died in his hesitancy before Macomb's earthworks as surely as the American lead balls had brought down Brock and Tecumseh. The war had destroyed Prevost, too, but for him there would be no monuments, no poetry and laudatory literature: only a recall to Britain under a cloud, and death short months later while waiting for a humiliating court martial. Two men chose to fight; one man chose not to fight; the war claimed all three as victims.

Robert Ross commanded the army that Rear Admiral Sir George Cockburn, reporting to Vice-Admiral Sir William Cochrane at Bermuda, transported into the Chesapeake. He had little difficulty brushing aside American resistance in the taking of Washington.

While these dramatic events were taking place on the inland battlefields of North America, the United States discovered, in the late summer of 1814, the full cost of declaring war on Great Britain – beyond the collapse of trade, the bankruptcy of the Treasury, and a failed attempt to take Canada. Major General Robert Ross was sent off in mid-summer, with just under three thousand infantry, to Bermuda. There he was joined by several thousand more, and embarked in a fleet under the command of Vice-Admiral Sir Alexander Cochrane, who had assumed command of the North American station. On August 3, the fleet sailed for the American coast, since Ross had instructions that were meant to make things easier for Prevost, and that instructed Ross to "effect a

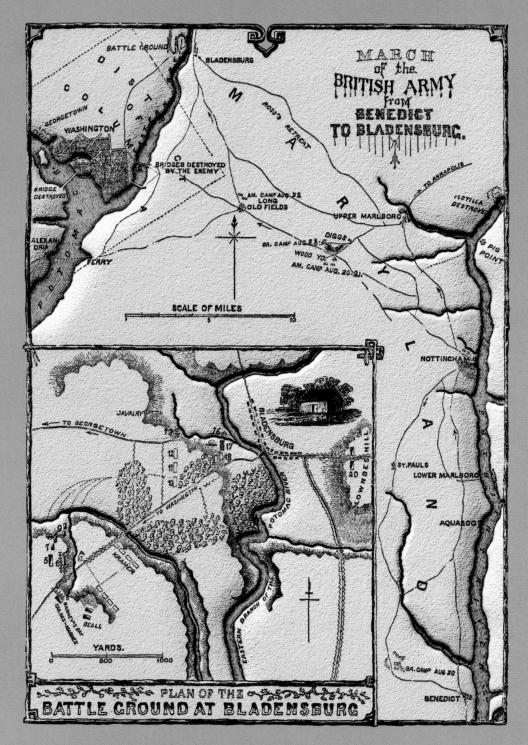

The British route to Washington and the disposition of the troops at Bladensburg, where an American force made up mostly of militia broke and ran after initial contact with the advancing British. The British, dusty and exhausted after their long march, declined to pursue the fleeing Americans, referring to their hasty retreat as the "Bladensburg Races."

diversion on the coasts of the United States of America in favour of the army employed in the defence of Upper and Lower Canada." Ross consulted with Cochrane, and the two settled on no small target indeed: the American capital city of Washington.

On August 15, Cochrane's fleet arrived in Chesapeake Bay, and entered the Patuxent River, finally halting at the small community of Benedict, Maryland. Here, four thousand infantry were ferried ashore in sweltering heat. The astonished and unprepared government in Washington now also reaped more of what George McClure had sown when Ross sent off a letter to James Monroe, secretary of state, saying that Ross's intentions were to "destroy and lay waste such towns and districts upon the coast as may be found assailable." As to why he was doing this, Ross said simply it was due to his "having been called upon by the Governor General of the Canadas to aid him in carrying into effect measures of retaliation against the inhabitants of the United States for the wanton destruction committed by their army in Upper Canada." Now British torches would be applied to McClure's own capital.

Final Stand at Bladensburg by Col. Charles Waterhouse. As the infantry defence collapsed at Bladensburg, American artillery made a valiant effort to slow the British advance, the only other noteworthy defence being put up by a party of United States Navy seamen under Joshua Barney. The British soon overcame this last resistance and marched unopposed on Washington.

(Above) Dolley Madison, wife of the president. She greeted the British attack with courage and spirit, narrowly avoiding capture as the British advanced, since she insisted on personally saving the well-known Gilbert Stuart portrait of George Washington (above, near right) from the White House. It now hangs in the National Portrait Gallery, Washington.

(Opposite, top) A contemporary illustration of British troops, accompanied by sailors, marching through Washington in 1814 and setting fire to public buildings, including the president's residence, in continuing retaliation for the burning of York's buildings by Dearborn's men, and the torching of Newark by McClure in 1813. Whitewashing of the president's residence after the fire led to it being known thereafter as the White House.

(Opposite, bottom) An American representation of the capture of Washington that portrays Ross's army deployed before the dramatically burning city. Far fewer buildings were actually set afire than the illustration suggests.

With the heat haze lying around it, the British column marched dustily through the village of Upper Marlboro to Bladensburg, a small community on the northeast edge of the District of Columbia. It was there that Ross ran into the only serious effort to stop him – when he came upon a larger force of mostly militia under Brigadier General William Winder, who had been captured in the Stoney Creek debacle. Winder's force appeared impressive, but almost without exception the Americans broke and ran when Ross's advance came at them with bayonets. Among them was President Madison, who had come out to inspire the troops. The honourable exception was a party of United States Navy seamen under Commodore Joshua Barney, who stood their ground and fought, with a courage that earned the admiration of the British, until they were overwhelmed. For the rest, the British characterized the American retreat as a foot race that the British were too tired to enter, being content to call them the "Bladensburg Races."

That evening Ross entered Washington, where, over the course of the night, the President's residence – later called the "White House," since it had to be whitewashed to hide the marks of burning – the Capitol, and other public buildings were burnt. There was less looting than might have been expected, unlike the experience at York, and Ross vacated the city on August 26 to march his dust-caked men back to the ships. The British regained Cochrane's vessels unmolested to any real degree, and the force sailed farther up the Chesapeake to the next target, Baltimore, Maryland.

Baltimore proved to be a far harder nut to crack. Its militia forces fought with tenacity and gave up ground bitterly, and the British suffered severe casualties in an unsuccessful bid to take the city – casualties that included Major General Ross. Another incident gave rise to the writing of what would become the American national anthem. A young American, Francis Scott Key, was detained aboard a British warship while the squadron unsuccessfully bombarded Fort McHenry, which sat on a point of land at the mouth of the Baltimore harbour. The fort was flying the Stars and Stripes from its tall flag mast as darkness fell, and through the night the British shelled the fort with the ships' guns and mortars, but also with great numbers of Congreve rockets, which whooshed skyward in a rush of flame, only to explode in flight when their warhead fuses burnt down. Scott was transfixed by the brave sight of the great, slowly rippling flag surrounded by drifting clouds of black powder smoke and lit with the lurid flicker of the rockets' trails and explosions. When light came, the flag still flew, and Key penned an admiring poem that would become "The Star-Spangled Banner." It was a fitting birth for the anthem of a nation that had been served by men of the quality of Winfield Scott, Oliver Perry, Joshua Barney, and Thomas Macdonough.

An American depiction of the death of Robert Ross outside Baltimore. American resistance, which had been negligible outside Washington, was far more stubborn at Baltimore and led to a British decision to withdraw following Ross's death.

While Cochrane effected his "diversions" at Washington and Baltimore, a smaller expeditionary force of just under two thousand men had embarked on ships at Halifax, Nova Scotia, and arrived in Penobscot Bay, Maine, on August 31, 1814. The British commander, Sir John Sherbrooke, used minimal force in taking the communities of Castine, Hampden, Bangor, and Machias. The British would retain possession of this part of Maine until the peace treaty restored it to the United States, and the British stay was marked with an amicability and mutual respect which brought home to both sides

BIRTH OF AN ANTHEM: THE ROCKETS ABOVE FORT McHENRY

When the British naval force reached Baltimore, it carried out an unsuccessful overnight bombardment of Fort McHenry, at the mouth of the harbour. The contemporary illustration (top) shows the anchored fleet beyond the fort, but firing mortar bombs which arc up and over to drop within the fort's walls. The British also used a far more spectacular weapon, the Congreve rocket. A contemporary illustration (bottom, left) shows a British warship firing Congreve rockets from ports set in the hull; the ports opened from slanting ramps built into the vessel's hold. The third contemporary illustration (bottom, right) shows how Congreves were also fired from small boats, employing a launching ramp attached to the boat's foremast. The crew shelter in the stern sheets of the boat as the weapon is fired. For sailing and rowing, the launching ramp and long-tailed rockets were lowered and stowed in the boat between the rowers. (Opposite) A young American lawyer, Francis Scott Key, was detained aboard one of the bombarding warships off Baltimore, and he was so moved by the sight of Fort McHenry's ensign flying amidst the drifting smoke and lurid light of the rockets that he penned the poem "The Star-Spangled Banner," which became the American national anthem.

that the war did not reflect the true feelings, inclinations, and wishes of the people on the northern Atlantic coast. Its civility contrasted with the brutal savagery of the frontier war in Upper Canada and Ohio country, and it presaged how the common people of North America would one day relate to one another peacefully, rather than on a bloodied battlefield.

On Christmas Eve, 1814, British and American commissioners signed a treaty at Ghent, Belgium, ending the war, but leaving all the major issues that gave rise to the war for later discussion and resolution.

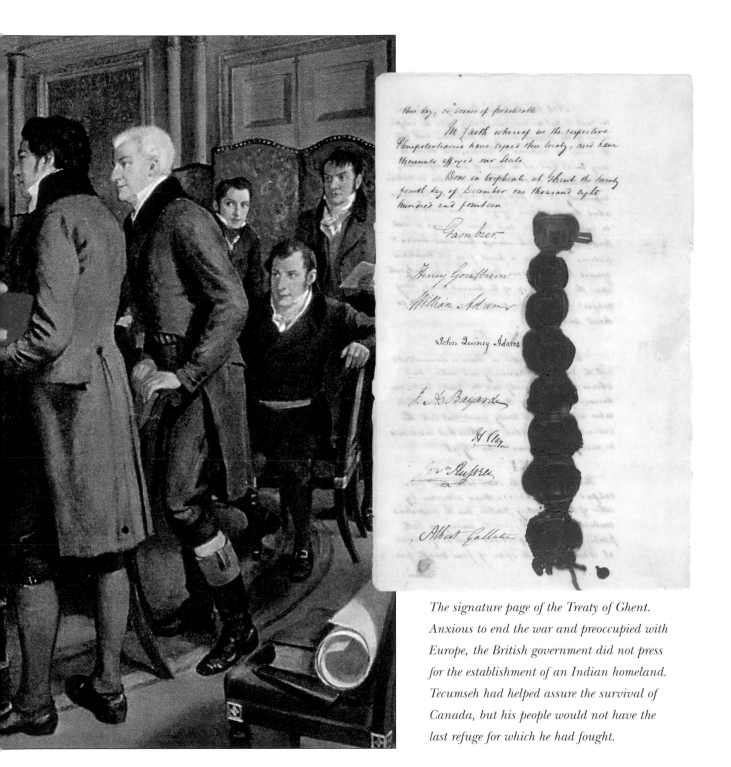

The signature page of the Treaty of Ghent. Anxious to end the war and preoccupied with Europe, the British government did not press for the establishment of an Indian homeland. Tecumseh had helped assure the survival of Canada, but his people would not have the last refuge for which he had fought.

On Christmas Eve, 1814, in Ghent, Belgium, a peace treaty that essentially restored things to where they had been before the war was quietly signed between Great Britain and the United States of America. All occupied lands were returned, all issues set aside for eventual discussion by later governments. There was no mention of free trade, nor of sailors' rights, and the British did not press for what Brock had promised, an Indian homeland. The Americans were pleased to get what they did in the treaty, which was helped by Prevost's failure and by Britain's war weariness. Each country left with a sense of having not lost, and eventually believed it had won. Only one party ended with nothing, and enjoyed no hint of victory – despite so many killed, so many homeless and displaced: the tribes who had followed Tecumseh into the struggle. In large part, he and they had saved the future Canada. But their own struggle for survival was only just beginning.

The new year, 1815, came with the promise of peace. No muskets banged or cannons roared on Canadian soil. Away to the south, at New Orleans, a foolish British commander wasted two thousand men in a lunatic assault on Andrew Jackson's marksmen, who sheltered behind their cotton bales on a foggy January morning. Jackson lost seventy-one men and began a rise that would take him to the White House. But in Canada, the killing, at last, was over.

A contemporary view of the Battle of New Orleans, fought on January 8, 1815, before news of the Treaty of Ghent had arrived. The British Army commander, Sir Edward Pakenham, ordered British troops into a frontal assault against a barricade line, behind which a mixed force of American defenders waited under the command of Andrew Jackson. Jackson's men, shown here on the left, fired from a protected position at the packed ranks of slowly advancing infantry, inflicted an appalling loss of over two thousand men on the British while losing only seventy-one of their own number. It was the worst British defeat of the war.

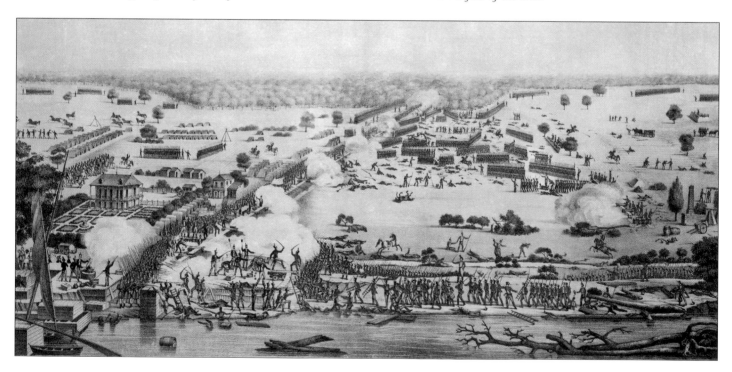

No WAR CAN BE CELEBRATED, or its achievements trumpeted. It is always a tragedy; the moment of the first death is one of human failure, not cause for rejoicing. But in the bloodletting and the clash of contentious forces and ideas, decisions are made and perceptions are altered that force change upon individuals and upon nations and create new realities. This was the ultimate effect of the War of 1812, which was in summary a ferocious and bitterly fought struggle that sprawled over a thousand-mile panorama of river, lake, forest, and tilled field, and gave two nations an enhanced sense of who they were or who they were not; gave a third a lesson on the limits of power; and brought about bitter and irredeemable loss for a fourth people, the Native tribes of eastern North America.

For the United States, the War of 1812 was several things: a flexing of muscle intended to force Great Britain into serious recognition of the new republic; an effort to sweep away British presence and take the arable lands of Canada at a time when the prairies were considered unfarmable; and, most important, an attempt to deal a death blow to the remaining Indian opposition, which, with British support, was hopelessly but bloodily resisting the American westward advance. This advance was proceeding with little regard for legality or treaty obligations, and the disparate tribes were united in the fear of their coming extinction. Ironically, their recourse to arms would deny the Americans the control of all North America that they once felt to be their natural destiny, and which might have been theirs had they not come north armed for battle.

For Great Britain, locked in endless struggle with France, the war was a tedious and irritating backwater conflict, which was taken more seriously only as the defeat of Napoleon loomed. The British chose to attend to the war with a meagre husbanding of resources and cautious conduct until the very end, and left it having experienced humiliation as well as success, and learned some limits of military and naval power.

For the Indian nations of the frontier who followed the charismatic leadership of Tecumseh, the war had seemed a heaven-sent opportunity in which an alliance with their "father over the sea" would allow them to check the American advance and establish a protected and recognized Indian homeland in eastern North America. It soon became a tragedy – and marked the shattering of Indian hopes in the east – even as their desperate resistance ensured, in large part, a future for Canada.

In the Canadian story, three figures stand out above the rest, two whose lives became the stuff of heroes, and one a cautious administrator, fearful of the hero's risk. The first two would die; the last would see out the war and retain Canada, but suffer for his caution. Each in turn contributed to Canada's survival. Each in turn suffered for that contribution, and was destroyed by it.

For the Canadas and their inhabitants as a whole, the war was a nightmarish awakening to the cost of a separate identity. To the Loyalists, still angry and resentful over their lost lives to the south, it was a return to the vicious and fratricidal fighting of 1775 to 1783, and it embedded in them a bitter opposition to all things republican and populist, including open democratic government, thereby sowing the seeds of future rebellion in the Canadas. To recent American immigrants taking up generous land grants, it was a moment of forced decision, in which they had to display and defend an uncertain new identity. And for the French in Lower Canada, it was another of the English civil wars in which they now had a demonstrable stake – and they fought well for that stake.

As these different groups in British North America silently surveyed the ruined farms and communities along Lake Erie, the Thames Valley, or the Niagara frontier, and the mass graves that held sons, fathers, and brothers, they might have had no clear sense of a common nationhood as yet; but they knew whom they were *not*, and it had been the bayonet and the torch that had forced this knowledge on them.

EYEWITNESSES TO THE WAR

A photograph taken in 1861 shows surviving Canadian veterans of the War of 1812 at a gathering in Toronto. These men may have seen and even known Isaac Brock and Tecumseh, and the courage and sacrifice of their contribution to the defence of Canada led to a belief that the Canadian militia had been primarily responsible for throwing back the American invasion. In reality the successful defence of Canada had been a partnership between the Indian warrior, the British regular soldier, and the Canadian militiaman. In their dogged struggle they jointly made possible the nation that came into being in 1867, six years after this photograph was taken.

AUTHOR'S NOTES ON SOURCES

As THIS BOOK was intended for general readership as a popular history rather than a work of academic scholarship, I have relied on secondary sources as guides in the writing of this book, save for the journal of Anne Prevost, a privately owned document that was made available through the kindness of Sabrina Matthews, researcher for the Galafilm/PTV television documentary of the war. In addition, to further the sense of a narrated story rather than an academic dissertation, the practice of footnoting was not employed, although I take away nothing from formal historians both able to tell a story well and to footnote it. The quotations from American members of Congress are almost without exception taken from secondary sources, which in turn recorded the statements of the men on the floor of Congress.

In addition to the appended bibliography of suggested further reading, prepared by Sabrina Matthews, the reader is directed to two detailed battle studies written as companion pieces by the fine Canadian military historian Donald E. Graves: *Field of Glory: The Battle of Crysler's Farm, 1813* (1999), and *Where Right and Glory Lead: The Battle of Lundy's Lane* (1997), both published by Robin Brass Studio; and to the study of the Royal Navy on Lake Ontario during the war by naval historian Robert Malcolmson, entitled *Lords of the Lake: The Naval War on Lake Ontario, 1812-1814* (1998), also by Robin Brass Studio. Along with John Sugden's superb biography *Tecumseh*, these works will best introduce the reader to the remarkable body of formal scholarship now available concerning the war, and provide a deeper understanding of what took place in that tragic conflict.

Victor Suthren
Ottawa, Ontario

BIBLIOGRAPHY

Compiled by Sabrina Matthews, senior researcher for the film documentary "War of 1812" (written by Brian and Terrance McKenna, produced by Galafilm and PTV Productions).

Allen, Robert S. *His Majesty's Indian Allies: British Indian Policy in the Defence of Canada, 1774-1815.* Toronto: Dundurn Press, 1992.

Antal, Sandy. *A Wampum Denied: Proctor's War of 1812.* Ottawa: Carleton University Press, 1997.

Barry, James P. *Old Forts of the Great Lakes: Sentinels in the Wilderness.* Lansing, MI: Thunder Bay Press, 1994.

Benn, Carl, et al. *War along the Niagara: Essays on the War of 1812 and Its Legacy.* Youngstown, NY: Old Fort Niagara Association, 1991.

Berton, Pierre. *The Invasion of Canada, 1812-1813.* Toronto: McClelland & Stewart, 1980.

Berton, Pierre. *Flames Across the Border, 1813-1814.* Toronto: McClelland & Stewart, 1981.

Brant, Irving. *James Madison: The President.* 6 volumes, Indianapolis: The Bobbs-Merrill Co., 1956.

Byfield, Shadrach. *Recollections of the War of 1812: Three Eyewitnesses' Accounts.* Toronto: Baxter Publishing Co., 1964.

Chartrand, René. *Uniforms and Equipment of the United States Forces in the War of 1812.* Youngstown, NY: Old Fort Niagara Association, 1992.

Cobb, Hubbard. *American Battlefields: A Complete Guide.* New York: Macmillan, 1995.

Dudley, William S., ed. *The Naval War of 1812: A Documentary History.* Washington: Naval Historical Centre, Department of the Navy, 1992.

Dunlop, William. *Tiger Dunlop's Upper Canada.* Toronto: McClelland & Stewart, 1967.

Dunnigan, Brian Leigh. *The British Army at Mackinac, 1812-1815.* Mackinac: Mackinac State Historic Parks, 1980.

Eckert, Allan W. *A Sorrow in Our Hearts: The Life of Tecumseh.* New York: Bantam Books, 1993.

Edmunds, R. David. *Tecumseh and the Quest for Indian Leadership.* Boston: Little, Brown and Co., 1984.

Elliott, James. *Billy Green and the Battle of Stoney Creek.* Stony Creek, ON.: Stoney Creek Historical Society, 1994.

Elting, John R. *Amateurs to Arms: A Military History of the War of 1812.* New York: Da Capo Press, 1995.

Esarey, Logan. *Messages and Letters of William Henry Harrison, Vols. 1 and 2.* New York: Arno Press, 1975.

Gleig, G. R. *The Campaigns of the British Army at Washington and New Orleans.* London: John Murray, 1836.

Hanks, Jarvis, Amasiah Ford, and Alexander McMullen. *Soldiers of 1814: American Enlisted Men's Memoirs of The Niagara Campaign.* Edited by Don Graves. Youngstown, NY: Old Fort Niagara Assoc., 1995 (Gala).

Hannon, Leslie F. *Forts of Canada: The Conflicts, Sieges, and Battles That Forged a Great Nation.* Toronto: McClelland & Stewart, 1969.

Heidler, David S. and Jeanne T. Heidler, eds. *Encyclopedia of the War of 1812.* Santa Barbara, CA: ABC-CLIO, 1997.

Hickey, Donald R. *The War of 1812: A Forgotten Conflict.* Urbana, IL: University of Illinois Press, 1990.

Klinck, Carl F., ed. *Tecumseh: Fact and Fiction in Early Records.* Ottawa: The Tecumseh Press, 1978.

LeCouteur, John. *Merry Hearts Make Light Days: The 1812 Journal of Lieutenant John LeCouteur, 104th Foot.* Edited by Donald E. Graves. Ottawa: Carleton University Press, 1993.

Lewis, Dennis M. *British Naval Activity on Lake Champlain During the War of 1812.* Plattsburgh, NY: Clinton County Historical Association, 1994.

Lossing, Benson J. *The Pictorial Field-Book of the War of 1812.* New York: Harper and Brothers, 1869.

The Dolley Madison Papers. Manuscript Division, Library of Congress, microfilm reel #1 (1794-1842).

Malcolmson, Robert and Thomas Malcolmson. *HMS Detroit: The Battle for Lake Erie.* St. Catharines, Ontario: Vanwell Publishing Inc., 1990.

Malcolmson, Robert. *Burying General Brock: A History of Brock's Monument.* Toronto: The Friends of Fort York, 1996.

Manning, William R., selected and arranged by. *Diplomatic Correspondence of the United States, Canadian Relations, 1784-1860, Vol. 1 (1784-1820)*. Washington: Carnegie Endowment for International Peace, 1940.

Marrin, Albert. *1812: The War Nobody Won*. New York: Atheneum, 1985.

Moore, Virginia. *The Madisons: A Biography*. New York: McGraw-Hill Book Company, 1979.

Moser, Harold D. et al., eds. *The Papers of Andrew Jackson, Vol. III, 1814-1815*. Knoxville: University of Tennessee Press, 1991.

Norton, John. *The Journal of Major John Norton*. Toronto: The Champlain Society, 1970.

Owsley, Frank Lawrence. *Struggle for the Gulf Borderlands: The Creek War and the Battle of New Orleans, 1812-1815*. Gainesville: University Presses of Florida, 1981.

Quaife, Milo Milton, ed. *War on the Detroit: The Chronicles of Thomas Verchères de Boucherville and the Capitulation*. Chicago: Lakeside Press, 1940.

Remini, Robert V. *Andrew Jackson and the Course of the American Empire, 1767-1821*. New York: Harper and Row, 1977.

Richardson, John. *Tecumseh: A Poem in Four Cantos*. London, ON: Canadian Poetry Press, 1992.

Scott, Winfield. *The Memoirs of Lieutenant General Scott, LL.D.* New York: Sheldon and Co., 1864.

Sheads, Scott. *Fort McHenry*. Baltimore: The Nautical and Aviation Publishing Company of America, 1995.

Sheppard, George. *Plunder, Profit, and Paroles: A Social History of the War of 1812 in Upper Canada*. Montreal: McGill-Queen's University Press, 1994.

Stanley, George F. G. *The War of 1812: Land Operations*. Canadian War Museum Publication No. 18. Toronto: Macmillan of Canada, 1983.

Sugden, John. *Tecumseh's Last Stand*. Norman, OK: University of Oklahoma Press, 1985.

Sugden, John. *Tecumseh: A Life*. New York: Henry Holt and Company, 1997.

Sword, Wiley. *President Washington's Indian War: The Struggle for the Old Northwest, 1790-1795*. Norman, OK: University of Oklahoma Press, 1985.

Tupper, Ferdinand Brock. *The Life and Correspondence of Major-General Sir Isaac Brock*. London: Simpkin, Marshall and Co., 1845.

Wohler, Patrick J. *Charles de Salaberry: Soldier of the Empire, Defender of Quebec*. Toronto: Dundurn Press, 1984.

PICTURE CREDITS

Pages 8-9   *See page 53.*

Page 11   *British Surrender at Yorktown, 1781*, artist unknown. Courtesy
                   of Beverley R. Robinson Collection, U.S. Naval Academy
                   Museum.

Page 13   *Canoes in a Fog*, by Frances Ann Hopkins. Glenbow
                   Museum, Calgary, AB. CN 55.81.1 PHN 468.

Page 14   *A View of the Launching Place above the Town of Quebec, 1759*,
                   by Francis Swaine. National Archives of Canada, C-002736.

Page 15   *The Death of General Wolfe, Quebec, 1857*, by Alonzo Chappel.
                   National Archives of Canada, C-042249.

Page 16   *Battle of Trafalgar, October 21, 1805*, engraved by W. Miller,
                   after painting by D. Standfield, R.A. Courtesy of Beverley R.
                   Robinson Collection, U.S. Naval Academy Museum.

Page 16   *Napoleon Bonaparte*, engraving by Laugier, after David, 1812.
                   Library of Congress, Washington, DC. LC-USZ62-17088.

Page 18   *Thomas Jefferson*, by Charles Willson Peale. Independence
                   National Historic Park, Philadelphia, PA.

Page 19   *Map of Eastern North America.* Courtesy of the William L.
                   Clements Library, The University of Michigan, Ann Arbor, MI.

Page 20   *"A scene on the frontier as practiced by the humane British and
                   their worthy allies,"* Philadelphia, 1812, by Wm. Charles,
                   del et Sculp. Library of Congress, Washington, DC.
                   LC-USZ62-5800.

Page 21   *Young Omahaw, War Eagle, Little Missouri, and Pawnees*,
                   by Charles Bird King. National Museum of American Art,
                   Smithsonian Institution, Washington, DC.

Page 22   *Henry Clay*, by Matthew Jouett. Diplomatic Rooms, U.S.
                   Department of State.

Page 108   *Tecumseh Saving Prisoners during Northwest Indian War,*
                engraving by Virtue & Co. Library of Congress,
                Washington, DC. LC-USZ62-46488.

Page 109   *Sir George Cockburn, GCB,* by C. Turner after J.J. Hall. Library
                of Congress, Washington, DC. LC-USZ62-12334.

Page 110   *"Admiral Cockburn burning and plundering Havre de Grace on
                the 1st of June 1813; done from a sketch taken on the spot at the
                time,"* artist unknown. Anne S. K. Brown Military Collection,
                Brown University Library.

Page 111   (Top) *The Pictorial Field-Book of the War of 1812,* Benson J.
                Lossing, coloured by Eric Grice & Andréa Hamel, Galafilm
                Multi-media, Montreal, QC.

Page 111   (Bottom) *American Soldier, 1814,* by H. Charles McBarron.
                Courtesy of the U.S. Army Center of Military History.

Pages 112-113 *43rd Regiment on March from New Brunswick to Canada, across
                Madawaska Portage, 1837,* by William Robert Herries.
                Courtesy of the Royal Ontario Museum, Toronto.

Page 114   (Bottom, left) *The Pictorial Field-Book of the War of 1812,*
                Benson J. Lossing, coloured by Eric Grice & Andréa Hamel,
                Galafilm Multi-media, Montreal, QC.

Pages 114-115 (Top) *Toronto, 1813,* by Owen Staples. Toronto Reference
                Library, J. Ross Robertson Collection, #T10271.

Page 115   (Bottom, right) *The Detonation of the Grand Magazine at York,*
                by Allan Robinson (1971.90.3). Courtesy of Toronto
                Historical Board.

Page 116   *The Pictorial Field-Book of the War of 1812,* Benson J. Lossing,
                coloured by Eric Grice & Andréa Hamel, Galafilm Multi-
                media, Montreal, QC.

Page 117   *The Taking of Fort George,* artist unknown. National Archives
                of Canada, C-006048.

Page 118   *Map of the Niagara Frontier.* Courtesy of the Westpoint
                Museum Collections, United States Military Academy
                Library, Westpoint, NY.

Page 119   *The* Hornet *Sinking the* Peacock, artist unknown. Courtesy
                of Beverley R. Robinson Collection, U.S. Naval Academy
                Museum.

Page 180   *A Sketch of the Battle of La Fourche, or Chateauguay*, by
                Bouchette, 1815. McCord Museum of Canadian History,
                Montreal, QC.

Page 181   Photograph by Vince Pietropaolo for *War of 1812*,
                TV documentary series produced by Galafilm Inc. and
                PTV Productions.

Page 182   *Colonel George Macdonnell, C.B.*, artist unknown. National
                Archives of Canada, C-019719.

Pages 184-185 *The Battle of Chateauguay*, by Baron Homfeldt de Dirckinck.
                Musée du Château Ramezay, Montreal, QC.

Page 186   *"Piquet de garde,"* by Eugene Leliepvre. Courtesy of Parks
                Canada/avec la permission de Parcs Canada.

Pages 188-189 *U.S. Infantry, October 1813*, by H. Charles McBarron. Courtesy
                of Parks Canada/avec la permission de Parcs Canada.
                Photo: Jean Jolin.

Page 190   *Rifle Corps in Action, 1813–1821*, by William Walton. From
                *The Army and Navy of the United States from the Revolution
                to the Present Day*, George Barrie, Publisher, 1889.

Page 191   *Field Officers and a Dragoon Private, 1810–1813*, by William
                Walton. From *The Army and Navy of the United States
                from the Revolution to the Present Day*, George Barrie,
                Publisher, 1889.

Page 192   *Infantry Skirmish Line Advancing, 1813–1816*, by William
                Walton. From *The Army and Navy of the United States from the
                Revolution to the Present Day*, George Barrie, Publisher, 1889.

Page 194   *Prescott, from Ogdensburg Harbor, New York, U.S.A., 1840*,
                by William Henry Bartlett. National Archives of Canada,
                C-002339.

Page 195   *Jacob Brown*, line and stipple engraving after painting by
                Alonzo Chappel. National Archives of Canada, C-100390.

Page 196   *The Pictorial Field-Book of the War of 1812*, Benson J. Lossing,
                coloured by Eric Grice & Andréa Hamel, Galafilm Multi-
                media, Montreal, QC.

Pages 198-199 *"Battle of Crysler's Farm,"* mural by Adam Sherriff Scott for
                the St. Lawrence Parks Commission/Upper Canada Village.
                (Also on pages 162-163.)

Page 220   *The Pictorial Field-Book of the War of 1812*, Benson J. Lossing, coloured by Eric Grice & Andréa Hamel, Galafilm Multimedia, Montreal, QC.

Page 221   *"Those Are Regulars, by God,"* by H. Charles McBarron. Courtesy U.S. Army Center of Military History.

Page 222   *Colonel Miller at the Battle of Chippewa*, by F. C. C. Darley. Anne S. K. Brown Military Collection, Brown University Library.

Page 224   *A View of the Running Fight*, by Peter Spicer. Courtesy of U.S. Naval Historical Center, Washington, DC.

Page 227   *The Pictorial Field-Book of the War of 1812*, Benson J. Lossing, coloured by Eric Grice & Andréa Hamel, Galafilm Multimedia, Montreal, QC.

Page 228   (Top) *The Battle of Niagara*, by William Strickland, after Major Riddle. Anne S. K. Brown Military Collection, Brown University Library.

Page 228   (Bottom) *The Battle of Lundy's Lane*, by Alonzo Chappel. National Archives of Canada, C-12093.

Page 229   (Bottom) *"Battle of Lundy's Lane, British Defending Cannons with Bayonets,"* by C. W. Jefferys. Courtesy of C. W. Jefferys Estate Archive, Toronto and City of Toronto Archives.

Page 231   *Arm Carried Off by Cannon Shot*, by Sir Charles Bell. Royal Army Medical Corps Museum, London, England.

Page 232   *Gunshot Wound Through Both Eyes*, by Sir Charles Bell. Royal Army Medical Corps Museum, London, England.

Page 233   *"Cutting Out" – Exploit 1814*, by C. H. J. Snider. Toronto Reference Library, J. Ross Robertson Collection, JRR 1163.

Pages 234-235   *Repulsion of the British at Fort Erie*, by E. C. Watmough. Chicago Historical Society, Chicago, IL.

Page 236   *The Pictorial Field-Book of the War of 1812*, Benson J. Lossing, coloured by Eric Grice & Andréa Hamel, Galafilm Multimedia, Montreal, QC.

Page 237   *Fort Erie Bastion Blown Up*, by A. Bobbett. National Archives of Canada, C-00023.

Page 238   *Lake Ontario Patrol, 1814*, by Peter Rindlisbacher. Courtesy of the artist.

Page 239   *Field Marshal, His Grace the Duke of Wellington*, KG & GCB, 1822, by William Beechey. National Archives of Canada, C-011791.

Page 254   (Top) *A View of the Bombardment of Fort McHenry*, by J. Bower, Philadelphia (original engraving). Courtesy of Beverley R. Robinson Collection, U.S. Naval Academy Museum. (Also on pages 204-205.)

Page 254   (Bottom, left) *Congreve's Rockets System (Plate 12)*, by Colonel William Congreve. Anne S. K. Brown Military, Collection Brown University Library.

Page 254   (Bottom, right) *Congreve's Rockets System (Plate 10)*, by Colonel William Congreve. Anne S. K. Brown Military Collection, Brown University Library.

Page 255   *The Star-Spangled Banner: Francis Scott Key Observing U.S. Flag from Deck of Sloop*, reproduction of painting by Percy Martin. Library of Congress, Washington, DC, LC-USZC4-6200.

Pages 256-257   *"A Hundred Years of Peace,"* by Amedée Forestier. National Archives of Canada, C-115678.

Page 257   *Treaty of Ghent, signature page.* William L. Clements Library, The University of Michigan, Ann Arbor, MI.

Page 258   *Battle of New Orleans*, by Hyacinth Laclotte. Historic New Orleans Collection, Kemper & Leila Williams Foundations, New Orleans, LA.

Page 260   *Survivors of the 1812 War*, photographer unknown. Ontario Public Archives, S1436, Toronto.

INDEX

Numerals in italics indicate illustrations.